TRENDS IN
BIOINFORMATICS RESEARCH

TRENDS IN BIOINFORMATICS RESEARCH

PETER V. YAN
(EDITOR)

Nova Science Publishers, Inc.
New York

NOTICE TO THE READER

The Publisher has taken reasonable care in the preparation of this book, but makes no expressed or implied warranty of any kind and assumes no responsibility for any errors or omissions. No liability is assumed for incidental or consequential damages in connection with or arising out of information contained in this book. The Publisher shall not be liable for any special, consequential, or exemplary damages resulting, in whole or in part, from the readers' use of, or reliance upon, this material.

This publication is designed to provide accurate and authoritative information with regard to the subject matter covered herein. It is sold with the clear understanding that the Publisher is not engaged in rendering legal or any other professional services. If legal or any other expert assistance is required, the services of a competent person should be sought. FROM A DECLARATION OF PARTICIPANTS JOINTLY ADOPTED BY A COMMITTEE OF THE AMERICAN BAR ASSOCIATION AND A COMMITTEE OF PUBLISHERS.

Library of Congress Cataloging-in-Publication Data
Available upon request

ISBN 1-59454-739-4

Published by Nova Science Publishers, Inc. ✦ New York

CONTENTS

Preface   **vii**

Chapter I   Computed Energetics of Macromolecules. Part II:
                   Functional Residues- from Amino Acid Sequence?   **1**
                   Ivan Y. Torshin

Chapter II   Family Classification and Integrative Analysis for
                   Protein Functional Annotation   **33**
                   Cathy H. Wu, Hongzhan Huang, Anastasia
                   Nikolaskaya, C. R. Vinayaka, Sehee Chung
                   and Jian Zhang

Chapter III   Bioinformatics Tools for Large-Scale Functional
                   Classification of Proteins – The InterPro Database   **59**
                   N. J. Mulder, T. K. Attwood, A. Bairoch, R. Apweiler,
                   A. Bateman, W. C. Barker, D. Binns, P. Bradley,
                   U. Das, W. Fleischmann, N. Harte, N. Hulo,
                   A. Kanapin, M. Krestyaninova, P. S. Langendijk-
                   Genevaux, V. Le Saux, D. Lonsdale, R. Lopez,
                   J. Maslen, J. McDowall, A. Mitchell, D. A. Natale,
                   A. N. Nikolaskaya, S. Orchard, E. Quevillon,
                   C. J. A. Sigrist, D. J. Studholme, C. H. Wu

Chapter IV   Protein Content in Chordate and Embryophyte
                   Genomes   **95**
                   Christian Roth, Matthew J. Betts and
                   David A. Liberles

Chapter V   Open Source, Open Formats, Open Data –
                 Democratizing Bioinformatics Research   **117**
                 Mads Wichmann Matthiessen

Index   **143**

Preface

In Chapter I, in the first part of this study, a unifying model of the macromolecular structure and function was proposed and verified using published biochemical and structural data. Such models are essential for post-genomic biology for characterization of the many of the novel genes. The method allows identification of many important functional residues from spatial structure of a protein or RNA. However, to obtain spatial structure requires purification, establishing the primary structure (sequence), crystallization, data collection and only then solving the three-dimensional structure of the molecule. In the second part, results of another molecular mechanics study are presented. It was shown that many functional residues of a protein can be relatively accurately predicted using amino acid sequence as the only input data. Thus, the unifying model can be applied not only to the spatial structures. Using only sequence and not using any data on the spatial structural organization of the protein (nor any biochemical information), up to 100% of important functional residues can be identified in proteins of various functions. It is important that this result was achieved without relying on any kinds of sequence similarities with known proteins. Thus, the method can be directly applied to amino acid sequence- one of the most important output data of the genomic projects.

As reported in Chapter II, the high-throughput genome projects have resulted in a rapid accumulation of predicted protein sequences, however, experimentally-verified information on protein function lags far behind. The common approach to inferring function of uncharacterized proteins based on sequence similarity to annotated proteins in sequence databases often results in over-identification, under-identification, or even misannotation. To facilitate accurate, consistent and rich functional annotation of proteins, PIR employs a classification-driven rule-based automated annotation method supported by a bioinformatics framework that provides data integration and associative analysis. The PIRSF classification system provides protein classification from superfamily to subfamily levels in a network structure to reflect evolutionary relationship of full-length proteins, including the preservation of domain architecture. Family-specific rules are manually defined to allow for conditional propagation of such annotation as functional site residues and protein names from characterized proteins to unknown proteins. The iProClass integration of protein family, function and structure data allows associative analyses of proteins. The integrative approach leads to novel prediction and functional inference for uncharacterized proteins, allows systematic detection of genome annotation errors, and provides sensible propagation and standardization of protein annotation.

In chapter III, the emerging field of Bioinformatics is bringing with it a plethora of tools for the analysis of vast quantities of data. Biology in the current era focuses on large-scale experiments to get more questions answered in the shortest time. Technological advances in the laboratory are facilitating this trend, however, scientists are no longer able to manually decode the incoming data. Data analysis methods now require automation, and Bioinformatics is providing the necessary resources for this to happen. Examples of projects that have increased their scale dramatically are the genome sequencing projects. They are churning out raw sequence data at an alarming rate, and the result is a need for automated sequence analysis methods. The analysis of protein sequences is possible through sequence similarity searches and more importantly through the use of "protein signatures". The latter are methods for diagnosing a domain or characteristic region of a protein family in a protein sequence. They are very powerful for automatic functional annotation of proteins. A number of protein signature databases have developed, each using a variation on the handful of signature methods available. These databases are most effective when used together, rather than in isolation. InterPro integrates the major protein signatures databases into one resource, adding to the signatures with annotation, protein 3D structure information and additional useful links. InterPro groups all protein sequences matching related signatures into entries, providing a useful means for large-scale automatic annotation of these proteins. This chapter describes the protein signature databases, their integration into InterPro, and the applications of InterPro in protein classification.

Chapter IV focuses on the study of protein structures' local conformations having a long history principally based on the analysis of the classical repetitive structures (i.e. α-helix and β-sheet), and also on the characterization of some particular structures in the coil state (e.g. turns). The secondary structures are interesting for describing the global protein fold, but miss all the orientations of the connecting regions and so neglect many particularities of the coil state.

In order to take these structural features into account we have identified a local structural alphabet composed of 16 folding patterns of five consecutive residues called Protein Blocks (PBs). Conversely to the secondary structures, the PBs are able to approximate every part of the protein structures. These PBs have been used both to describe precisely the 3D protein backbones with an average *rmsd* of 0.42 Å, and to perform a local structure prediction with a rate of correct prediction of 48.7%.

In this chapter, we present the interest of the Protein Blocks by comparing the secondary structure assignment with the assignment in terms of PBs. We highlight the discrepancies between different secondary structure assignment methods and show some interesting correspondence between particular local folds and the Protein Blocks. Then, we use the Protein Block prediction to classify proteins into the classical structural classes, namely all α, all β and mixed. The prediction rate of theses different classes are good, i.e. 71.5%, with no confusion between all α and all β classes. Finally, we present a new approach named TopKAPi that stands for "Triangular Kohonen Map for Analyzing Proteins". It enables us to classify and analyze proteins according to their Protein Block frequencies using for this purpose a novel unsupervised clustering method: a triangular self-organizing Kohonen map. This method enables us to determine new relationships between local structures and amino acid distributions. This new methodology could be of great interest in proteomics and sequence alignment.

In chapter V, the advantages of open formats and open source software are described and relevant software for creating biocomputing platforms and networks are suggested. Bioinformatics research has developed at a rapid pace throughout the last decade. While the applications available at the end of the last century were mostly developed as tools for assisting regular molecular biologists or epidemiologist, more recently, the sequencing of several genomes, the large roll out of DNA microarray analysis equipment, and development of high throughput screening methods have required that software is developed to assist in bioinformatics analysis of the tremendous amounts of data produced by these methods. For the most part, these highly specialized software packages have been developed commercially and have - only been available at a premium cost. However, maturation of the laboratory technologies as well as the introduction and proliferation of open source software development in most categories of software (microarray expression analysis, genome analysis, office applications, graphics manipulation and advanced statistical analysis) has leveled the playing field in such a way that bioinformatics research is now available to anyone with a contemporary computer and an Internet connection. The parallel development of open data formats (most importantly XML) has had the similarly important implication that it is now possible to use different software applications to analyse the same data natively, such that firstly, applications compete on their quality and not on monopoly, and secondly, that the data is independent of the survival of specific software companies.

In: Trends in Bioinformatics Research
Editor: Peter V. Yan, pp. 1-32

ISBN 1-59454-739-4
© 2005 Nova Science Publishers, Inc.

Chapter I

Computed Energetics of Macromolecules. Part II: Functional Residues- from Amino Acid Sequence?

Ivan Y. Torshin[*1, 2]

[1]Federal Science Center (VEI), Moscow, Russia
[2]Bioinformatics Consulting, LLC, Moscow, Russia

Abstract

In the first part of this study, a unifying model of the macromolecular structure and function was proposed and verified using published biochemical and structural data. Such models are essential for post-genomic biology for characterization of the many of the novel genes. The method allows identification of many important functional residues from spatial structure of a protein or RNA. However, to obtain spatial structure requires purification, establishing the primary structure (sequence), crystallization, data collection and only then solving the three-dimensional structure of the molecule. In the second part, results of another molecular mechanics study are presented. It was shown that many functional residues of a protein can be relatively accurately predicted using amino acid sequence as the only input data. Thus, the unifying model can be

---

[*]E-mail: tiy135@yahoo.com

applied not only to the spatial structures. Using only sequence and not using any data on the spatial structural organization of the protein (nor any biochemical information), up to 100% of important functional residues can be identified in proteins of various functions. It is important that this result was achieved without relying on any kinds of sequence similarities with known proteins. Thus, the method can be directly applied to amino acid sequence- one of the most important output data of the genomic projects.

Introduction

Undoubtedly, establishing the genetic, physiological and cellular functions of product(s) of a novel gene (in particular, of a protein) is the task of the primary importance for characterization of any novel gene. The high through-put methods of functional genomics [1] will definitely be the main tool of the endeavor to understand more fully the function of each and every gene in a biological organism. Nevertheless, without biochemical and biophysical characterization of the gene product (whether it is protein or an RNA), the understanding of gene function will remain too general for any practical application, such as directed mutagenesis, protein design, drug design as well as many other biomedical applications.

The most important biochemical and biophysical characterization of any protein lies in the establishing the most important functional residues: catalytic and substrate-binding residues in enzymes, residues of protein-protein interactions, ligand-binding and other types of the functional residues. In the first part of this study, a unifying model for identification of the functional residues from a spatial structure of a protein or RNA was proposed and analyzed. Results of the energy calculations, both in proteins and RNA allowed relatively accurate prediction of the functional sites in most of the proteins of very different biochemistry and structure (enzymes, proteins involved in protein-protein interactions, metal, DNA-, hem- and fatty-acid binding proteins). On average, 72% of the topmost destabilizing residues and 64% of the topmost stabilizing residues of the proteins were either known functional residues or were spatially clustered around the known functional site regions. On average for the set of ribozymes, 70% of the least stabilizing nucleotides were either known to be functional or were less than 4.0 angstrom from the known functional residues. Thus, this unifying physico-chemical model, based on the fundamental laws of the physics and chemistry, has a potential for bringing together biochemical, biophysical and physico-chemical descriptions of the protein function. The postulate of the relativity of the energies of the functional residues, formulated in the 1st part of this study, allows differentiation between important functional residues and the rest of the residues in the protein. In the 1st part, this postulate was applied to a number of proteins with known spatial structure. However, it is not the case for most of the proteins with known sequences.

Apart from the scarcity of the proteins with solved spatial structures, analyses of the human genome show that only 50-60% of the proteins in the human genome can be functionally annotated using sequence similarity methods even of an advanced kind (such as described in [2]). In addition, sequence similarity search of any kind is rather a general method of annotation. A method that would allow reliable predictions of the functional residues from the amino acid sequence will be definitely helpful in the process of characterization of any novel protein. There are at least 40% of the novel proteins in the human genome. If such a method would be largely independent on the data on sequence identity, then it could be applied to an entirely novel protein. At least, the unifying model based on the relativity postulate (see 1st part) allows to propose such a unique sequence-based method. To formulate the idea of the method, it is important to consider which structural factors contribute to the stabilizing or destabilizing properties of the residues in the three-dimensional structure.

There are four conventional levels of considering the protein structure: primary (amino acid sequence), secondary (helices, strands, and turns/loops), tertiary (three-dimensional structure of a single subunit) and quaternary (organization of two or more subunits into a macromolecular complex). This categorization into levels of structure can sometimes be confusing and there are, of course, intermediate levels between these four levels (such as super-secondary structure). Nevertheless, such a classification (Figure 1) is of a great use for the analysis of the structural factors contributing to the relative energies of the individual residues. That is to say, one needs to consider the contribution of each of the levels of the protein structure to the energies of the residues.

```
smtdllsaedikkaigaftaadsfdhkkffqmvglkkksaddvkkvfhil
dkdksgfieedelgsilkgfssdardlsaketktlmaagdkdgdgkigve
efstlvaes
```

Figure 1a

```
1      SMTDLLSAEDIKKAIGAFTAADSFDHKKFFQMVGLKKKSADDVKKVFHIL        50
       LHHHHLLHHHHHHHHHHHLLLLLLLLHHHHHHHHHLLLLLLHHHHHHHHHH

51     DKDKSGFIEEDELGSILKGFSSDARDLSAKETKTLMAAGDKDGDGKIGVE       100
       LLLLLSSSSHHHHHHHHHHHHHLLLLLLLLHHHHHHHHHHHHLLLLLLSSSHH

101    EFSTLVAES                                                109
       HHHHHHHHL
```

Figure 1b

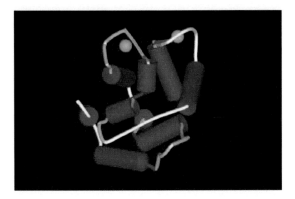

Figure 1c

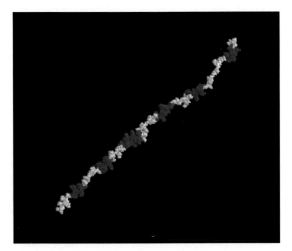

Figure 1d

Figure 1. Levels of protein structure, on the example of parvalbumin. a) Primary structure. The charged residues in the sequence are marked: positively charged (blue), negatively charged (red) and hydrophobic (white) residue types are indicated. It can be seen that there are clusters of the residues of the same charge. Calculations show that only some of these sequence clusters are destabilizing and even fewer are the most destabilizing. b) Secondary structure, "H" stands for alpha-helix, "S" for beta-strand and "L" for loops/turns. The secondary structure was derived using STRIDE software. c) Tertiary structure. This protein acts as a monomer thus quaternary structure is identical to the tertiary. Secondary structure elements are indicated, the large spheres are calcium ions. d) The most extended conformation: the spatial representation of the secondary structure of a protein. The helices are in red, as in figure c).

Primary structure (1D, Figure 1a) is the most important determinant of the secondary and the tertiary/quaternary structure of a protein. Some functional regions, such as phosphorylation sites, catalytic sites of well-characterized types and other known specific sites can be identified directly from sequence using well established sequence patterns, such as collected in PROSITE [3]. As the results of the present study will show (see below), the clusters of the charged residues remarkably often contain the known functional residues. However, the results also show that such sequence clusters of the charged residues are far from being the only factor determining the relative energies and, therefore, the functional properties of the individual residues. The primary structure does not bring any other structural restraint except the precise sequence of the residues of the definite types. Therefore, the energy values of individual residues will vary greatly depending on the particular conformation of the sequence. On the level of the secondary structure (2D, Figure 1b), some of the residues adjacent in the sequence are brought closer (in a turn or in an alpha-helix), some others are made further apart (the even/odd residues in the beta-strands). In the secondary structure, certain structural restraints appear: namely, the fixed geometry of the helices and the strands. These structural restraints will reduce variability in the energies of the individual residues when conformation of the polypeptide with the fixed secondary structure changes. Indeed, the results of calculations using the random organizations of the secondary structure elements (see Results & Discussion) show that the most destabilizing residues are the most destabilizing in many of the random conformations, if the secondary structure is fixed. In the tertiary structure (3D, Figure 1c), the residues from different parts of the sequence are brought together in the functional site of the protein (Ca-binding site in the case of the parvalbumin protein). The conformations of the folded proteins are remarkably rigid (especially in the case of enzymes where precise angstrom-level geometry is required for the efficient catalysis). The relative per-residue energies are determined, in particular, by the spatial arrangement of the residues on the molecular surface of the folded protein and, in particular, in the functional site.

Thus, going from the tertiary level of the structure to the primary structure, a residue can destabilize a tertiary structure either through 1. An unfavorable tertiary packing (3D) on the molecular surface and/or through 2. Destabilizing elements of secondary structure (2D). Both of these factors are determined by the primary structure (1D, i.e., amino acid sequence). It is extremely important to notice that the calculations on the tertiary structure (1st part of this study) were not designed to distinguish between the two above-mentioned cases (2D and 3D). It may quite happen that the primary determinant of whether a particular residue would be most destabilizing or the stabilizing is the destabilization or stabilization provided by the secondary (and not the tertiary) level structure. Therefore, an additional study needs to be designed and performed to assess the relative contribution of each of the levels of structure to the relative energetic properties of the residues.

Perhaps, the most reliable way to assess the relative energetical contributions provided at the level of the secondary structure is to eliminate the tertiary structure but to preserve the secondary structure. This can be easily done by putting into one line all of the elements of the secondary structure (Figure 1b) while maintaining the secondary structure by fixing the phi/psi angles of each residue. Such conformation of protein would correspond to an intermediate stage during protein folding (see Results & Discussion) [4]. Throughout the rest of this article, this conformation is referred to as "the most extended conformation" (Figure 1d).

Technically, the contributions of the individual residues to the protein stability were calculated using electrostatic and van der Waals terms, using the same procedure explicitly described in the part I of this article. The procedure of generating the most extended conformation is described in Methods.

Data and Methods

Protein Structures

The main set of the proteins analyzed was already described in Table 1 of the 1st part of this article. The results for this set are presented in the Tables 2&3. Some additional proteins were selected from PDB (Table 4), the relevant references are provided in the table.

Secondary Structure Definitions and Prediction

The secondary structure was derived from the proteins' tertiary structures using STRIDE [5]. The secondary structure was predicted from sequence using PsiPred [6] and the helix predictions confirmed using another method [7]. The reliability of the secondary structure predictions was calculated using standard Q3(total) formula [8].

The Most Extended Conformation

The initial unfolded conformation was constructed with phi=-160, psi=+160 for loops, phi=-50, psi=-41 for alpha-helices and phi=-120, psi=+90 for beta-strands. A general difficulty in the construction of the model structures is the flexibility of the side-chains that leads to various "rotamers" of a side-chain of a single type. The side chain conformations were generated using BPMC algorithm that was implemented in ICM [9] and as described in [7]. For each rotamer configuration of the fragment, van der Waals constraints and packing density were found. Then the optimal configuration of the entire most extended conformation was subjected to the molecular mechanics procedure (described in the 1st part of this study).

Results & Discussion

First of all, the overall comparison of results of the calculations on 3D (tertiary) and 2D (secondary) structures is made (Table 1). Secondly, analysis of the functional properties of the most destabilizing and the most stabilizing residues identified in the calculations on 2D structures is presented (Tables 2&3). Then the results of application of the method to an additional set of proteins are described (Table 4) and charge clusters in sequence were analyzed (Table 5). The predictions of the functional residues from sequence alone are followed up by the discussion of the choice of the extended conformation. Finally, the relative roles of the of the secondary/tertiary structures in relation to the protein synthesis, folding and function are considered.

Table 1. Summary of the most destabilizing and the most stabilizing residues in the 3D and 2D calculations. The residues were taken into account irrespectively of their functional properties. The proteins are ordered alphabetically. The total numbers of the identified residues are given detailed data on the particular residues and their functional properties are given in the Tables 1, 3&4 in 1st part of this study and in the Tables 2&3 of this, the 2nd, part

Protein	n(most destabilizing residues)			n(most stabilizing residues)		
	3D	2D	common residues	3D	2D	%common residues
ABP	9	9	1 (11%)	7	9	3 (43%)
APase	10	9	0 (0%)	11	12	0 (0%)
barnase	8	7	3 (44%)	8	10	6 (75%)
barstar	8	10	6 (75%)	6	9	6 (100%)
calbindin	8	10	6 (75%)	6	6	6 (100%)
cellulase E2	9	7	4 (44%)	10	10	4 (40%)
CRO protein	8	7	4 (50%)	7	7	4 (57%)
Cu SOD	10	10	2 (20%)	9	10	7 (78%)
Cytochrome P450	9	11	4 (44%)	9	10	4(44%)
Dhfr	7	10	6 (86%)	11	9	3 (27%)
Elastase	7	9	3 (43%)	10	10	10 (100%)
Fe SOD	5	9	1 (20%)	8	1	1 (13%)
i-fabp	7	10	7 (100%)	7	6	0(0%)
Ldh	7	10	4 (57%)	8	9	2(20%)
l-fabp	8	10	2 (20%)	7	9	1 (14%)
m-fabp	10	8	1 (10%)	9	9	4 (44%)
Myoglobin	10	10	5 (50%)	8	10	0 (0%)
parvalbumin	8	6	6 (75%)	8	10	5 (63%)
Pgm	9	8	3 (30%)	11	10	5 (45%)
Pla2	7	7	1 (14%)	8	8	4 (50%)
Pmi	10	10	1 (10%)	8	9	3 (38%)
ras protein	9	9	4 (44%)	6	9	3 (50%)
Snase	9	10	3 (30%)	10	9	5 (50%)
Tpi	7	6	1 (14%)	8	9	1 (13%)
On average			3 (42%)			3 (43%)

Table 2. The most destabilizing residues from the secondary-structure-only calculations on the proteins (in alphabetical order). "Efficiency 1,2" were calculated as in the Tables 3&4 of the 1st part

Protein	Residues with known function	residues adjacent to the functional site	False positives (no known function)	% efficiency 1	% efficiency 2
ABP	Q11	P12 P41 T65 P68 P256	V103 E276 P277 P278	50	10
APase	D327 AB: E406 D408 E411	E407 330	E341 D344 D346 E347	60	40
Barnase	K66	P21 A46	L20 P47 L63 P64	43	14
Barstar	E33 D36 D40 E77 E81	E29 E47	E24 E53	67	56
Calbindin	D19 D54 D58 E60 E65	E51	D47 E48 E52	67	56
cellulase E2	E263 D265	E115 W193 D233	E132 D249	71	29
CRO protein	K27 Q28 R41 P42 R43	-	K14 D55 P56	63	63
Cu SOD	H47 H49	E50 D53 E79 D102	D91 D93 D97 E101	60	20
cytochrome P450	E91 E94 H355	D97	D25 E152 D153 E172 R342 K344 H361	36	18
Dhfr	L54 P55	P21 P25	Q65 P66 P105 E129 D131	44	22
Elastase	H43	R226	R36 R51 S140 G205 H218	29	14
Fe SOD	D156 H160	E21 E24 E159	H17 E48 E87 D165	56	22
i-fabp	S71 D74	G22	K29 G44 D67 G75 G86 G99 G110	33	20
Ldh	N138	D82 D195 L198	E55 D84 D85 D88 I210	44	11
l-fabp	N24 S53 N54	Y14 K16 T76	F17 F68 Y70	67	33
m-fabp	V38 G76	F15 E72	C69 L71 V101 D107	50	25
Myoglobin	H64 H93 H97	H36 K96 K102	K50 K77 K87 H119	67	30
Parvalbumin	E59 D90 D92 D94	D61 E100	-	100	67
Pgm	K56 H181	-	K103 K108 P120 E214 D216	29	29

Pla2	E46 D49	T36 E40 D42	P18 D39	71	29
pmi	E138	P353	D35 D126 E167 E170 F338 P339 G380	22	11
ras protein	E31 D33 E37 D54 E62	D30 D57	D47 E49	78	56
snase	K49 K84 R87	K48 K53 K110 K116	K127 K133 K136	70	30
tpi	L80	P168 K239	P58 T179 P180	50	17
Total percentages (average for the set)				55%	30%

Table 3. The most stabilizing residues from the secondary-structure-only calculations on the proteins (in alphabetical order)

Protein	Residues with known function	residues adjacent to the functional site	False positives (no known function)	% efficiency 1	% efficiency 2
ABP	K10	K22	K26 K45 D157 K197 K242 K262 S273	22	11
APase	K328 H331 H412 AB: D28 R62	K127	K137 E193 K312 R351 K357 K358	50	42
barnase	K27 D54 E60 E73	D75 D93 D101	K19 E29 D86	70	40
barstar	-	N19 K22 R76 K79	R12 D16 K23 R55 K61	44	0
calbindin	-	K16 K25 K55	K12 K29 K41	50	0
Cellulase E2	R78 R237 K259	E15 R192	R18 D31 K202 R214	56	33
CRO protein	Q17	E35 E47	M15 L20 I34 F46	42	14
Cu SOD	R80 R116	R70 K71 K123 K137	K24 K76 K92 K129	60	20
Cytochrome P450	-	R109 K178 K197 R290	R79 R90 R130 R143 R161 R186	40	0
Dhfr	Y111 H114	W30	R33 E48 R98 H124 H141	38	25
Elastase	E74 H75 E84 D202	D63 E65 D108	D169 D193	79	44

Fe SOD	-	K29 R170	K43 K50 R57 K91 K107 R167	25	0
i-fabp	E15 F17	E19 L38 F47 R56	-	100	33
ldh	R169	K57 K112	K69 R87 R228 R283 R299 K311	33	11
l-fabp	G31 H33 D34 N57	K27 K92 E120	K20 M84	78	44
m-fabp	A21 V58 R126	F18 K78 G106 T112	L65 K96	78	33
myoglobin	-	D44 D60 E85 E105 E136	D27 E52 E54 E59	56	0
parvalbumin	-	K54 K68 K91 K96	K12 K13 D25 D41 D42 R75	40	0
Pgm	D50 E86	E34 E40 E44 D96	D24 D91 E99 E107	60	20
Pla2	R43 H48 R53 K56 E92	D99	K62 K87	75	63
pmi	K136 R304	K128 K282 K310	K20 K185 R227 K347 K404	50	20
ras protein	R41 K88	K42 R68 R73	E126 D132 D154	63	25
snase	L36 V39 D40 E43 D83	Y91	E101 E122 E129	67	56
tpi	W12 R98 Y102	V109	F28 Q132 E133 R138	50	38
Total percentages (average for the set)				55%	25%

Table 4. Calculations of the most extended conformation applied to another set of proteins. The proteins are ordered according to the fold class and size. The fold classes are indicated as aa for all alpha, bb for all beta, a+b and a/b indicate mixed alpha and beta folds. PPI, protein-protein interactions. For enzymes, the catalytic residues are marked with "(c)". For MHC subunits, groove indicates the residues of the major groove, and AB or BA indicate subunit-subunit contacts forming the groove. CAP sequence was subdivided into the cAMP-binding domain and the DNA-binding domain

protein	PDB, chain	fold	size	biochemistry	The most destabilizing residues		
					known functional residues	adjacent to the functional site	"false positives"
CAP, DNA	1run A	aa	71	DNA-binding [25]	K166 R169 R180 R185 K188	E191 E171	D155
Colicin E9	1bxiA	aa	85	PPI [26]	D26 E30 E32 Y55 D62	E42	E45 D60
CytC5	1cc5_	aa	87	heme-binding [27]	M63 P64 N55 K46 R42 W39 A30 K32	K17 E76 D50 K40	D13 D71 D74
CytC'	1jafA	aa	128	heme-binding [28]	N13 E70 W76	G60 K72 D124 K120 K88 D87 K83 E114	K101 I108 F105 P35
bcl-2	1g5m_	aa	166	PPI,apoptosis [29]	M115 S117 E114 D111 A113	E152	E29 E165 P168 D171 D191
subtilisin	2st1E	a/b	275	Protease [30]	D32 H64	D99 D60	D41
CI2	1ciqA	a+b	64	PPI [31][32]	L32 P33 E41 R46 R48	V60	E15 K17 D23 E26
FixL	1ew0 A	a+b	120	heme-binding [33]	R214 R208 K207 H194 F226	P189 P187 N181 D195 N199 K229 T150	N219 R220 N163 N169 E174 R241
lysozyme	1hel	a+b	129	Hydrolase [34]	E35(c) D52(c) N57	D48 N41	R112
HPPK	1hka	a+b	158	PPO4-kinase [35]	D97(c) H115(c)	E67 E77	E30 D52 E68 K85
MHC-A	1jk8A,	a+b	181	PPI, MHC II [36]	groove:K75 R76 R53 R52 H24	-	D171 E166

		bb			W43 E31 K67 R50, AB:N21 D27 D29 E30 E25		D162 D157 E159
MHC-B	1jk8B	a+b, bb	192	PPI, MHC II [36]	groove:W61 E74 N64 R70 E59, BA: E86 L53 P52 P56 P55 R29 R25 D152 D121 R93	-	E162 K128 E130 E137 W131 D135 D169 H174 T145
GBP	2gbp	a+b	309	galactose-binding [37]	D14 D134 E149 H152 D154 D190 D236	D13 D44 E156	D27 D33 D40 D50 E165 D179
6dLDL	1f8zA	Irr	39	Ca-binding [38]	D33 E34 D23 E25	-	N9 E7
BPTI	1cbwD	Irr	58	PPI [39]	K15 R17 R39	R20 K41	E7 K26 R42
SH3	1b07A	bb	58	PPI [40]	E149 D150 P183	E148 E167	R160 E173 D174
HIV-1pr	1dazC	bb	99	Protease [41]	R8 D25(c) D29 D30 P81	E34	R41 K55 D60
BMP-2	1es7A	bb	103	PPI [42]	K15 D53 H54 N68 V70 S69	D93 E94	K11
MFB2	1mdc_	bb	131	Fatty-acid binding [43]	A22 R127 N39 K105 L24 D77	K20 R126	W121 D27 K59 D46 D110
a-lbp	1adl_	Bb	131	Lipid-binding [44]	D76 T29 Q95 E72 R106	K37 G26 K105 D76	K100 K79 D87 K112 R108 E61 D71
CAP, cAMP	1run A	Bb	136	cAMP-binding [25]	E72 R123	D68 E78	R103 R115 R122

**Table 5. Calculations of the most extended conformation applied to several
ion channels. The residues predicted for ion channels are classed as forming
the main pore, inter-subunit contacts, or other sites (Ca1-3 calcium-binding
sites in annexin). See text of the article for details**

Protein	PDB	Chain size	Main pore	Inter-subunit contacts	Other sites	adjacent to the pore	"false positives"
Annexin xii 6mer	1aei A	316	E133	R23 E163 D173 E163 R269 K265 E142	Ca1:E105 Ca3:E70 Ca5:D301	E142 E172	D305 E182 D110 E210
CLC	1kpl _A	473	F269 A396 E148 R126 R123 D278 E111	I227 K216 Q460 D457 E117 D417		R169	I261 L305 F262 K131 S271
MSCL	1msl A	109	R98 K99 E104	L92 P93 E104 D108 Q51 Q105		D53	P106

Comparison of the Calculations on the Tertiary Structures and on the Most Extended Conformations

It should be underlined that the overall comparison was made irrespectively of the functional properties of the individual residues (Table 1). On average, 42% of the most destabilizing residues and 43% of the most stabilizing residues were the same in calculations using the tertiary structure (which is fully folded and compact protein) and the most extended conformation (which is extended and represents only the secondary structure). In some proteins both the most destabilizing and the most stabilizing residues appear to be primarily determined by the tertiary structure (APase, FeSOD, tpi and l-fabp). In several other proteins only the most destabilizing residues (Pla2, ABP, m-fabp, pmi and CuSOD) or only the most stabilizing residues (myoglobin and i-fabp) were determined mostly by the tertiary structure. Thus, it can be said that the average contribution of the secondary structure to the energetical properties of individual residues is roughly 40%-50%. Consequently, the average contribution of the tertiary structure to the individual energetical differences between the residues would be 50%-60%. The results make clear that the secondary structure is an important factor in determining the relative energies of the individual residues.

Therefore, it is quite possible that at least some of the most destabilizing residues and some of the most stabilizing residues in the tertiary structure (3D) could also be identified using only the secondary structure (2D)- that is, by applying the calculations to the most extended conformations.

Functional Residues Identified in Calculations on the Most Extended Conformation

Indeed, 55% (on average) of the destabilizing residues (Table 2) and also 55% of the most stabilizing residues (on average, Table 3) in 2D calculations were either functional or were spatially clustered (6-8 angstrom) around the known functional sites. The result is quite remarkable, taking into account that only secondary structure was used. In a few proteins (pmi, elastase, barnase, tpi) only one of the most destabilizing residues was known to be functional. In some proteins (parvalbumin, FeSOD, cytochrome P450, calbindin, myoglobin, barstar and CRO protein) one or less of the most stabilizing residues were known to be functional. Only in two proteins both the most destabilizing and the most stabilizing residues with known function were few (ABP and LDH). In calculations on the tertiary structure (see part I, Tables 3&4) the functional most destabilizing residues were few in snase, dhfr and i-fabp while the functional most stabilizing residues were few in CRO protein, calbindin, barstar, parvalbumin and Fe SOD (remarkably, almost the same set of proteins as in the 2D calculations). Only in P450-cytochrome and LDH (lactate dehydrogenase) most of the known functional residues were neither most destabilizing nor the most stabilizing. Therefore, lactate dehydrogenase (and, to some extent, also P450 cytochrome) appears to be the only exclusion from the relativity postulate (among the proteins analyzed). It is quite possible, however, that the most destabilizing and the most stabilizing residues in this protein have yet unknown function.

There seems to be no distinct correlation between the percentage of the common residues in 2D/3D calculations (as summarized in the Table 1) and the percentage of the known functional residues identified. The proteins with the most destabilizing residues being determined largely by the tertiary structure were Pla2, ABP, m-fabp, pmi and CuSOD. At the same time, the analysis of the functional significance shows that less than two of the most destabilizing residues were known to be functional in other subset of the proteins (pmi, elastase, barnase, tpi) and PMI enzyme is the only common protein between the two above-mentioned subsets. At the same time, the proteins with the most stabilizing residues being determined largely by the tertiary structure were myoglobin and i-fabp while the functional analysis given above shows another subset of the proteins (parvalbumin, FeSOD, cytochrome P450, calbindin, myoglobin, barstar and CRO protein), myoglobin being is the only common protein. Thus, the residues that were identified both in between in 2D and 3D calculations are not always functional.

Let's consider the results for a few proteins in a greater detail. In parvalbumin (Figure 1), the known functional residues are D51, D53, S55, E59, E62, D90, D92, D94, and E101 [10]. Calculations using the tertiary structure (PDB 1rtp) show that 7 out of these 9 residues excluding D51 and S55 were the most destabilizing (Asp51 was among the destabilizing). The amino acid sequence contains two large sequence clusters of the negatively charged residues (59-62 and 90-94, Figure 1a) that include the functional residues. These charged clusters will be discussed later. In the most extended conformation 4 out of the 9 residues (E59, D90, D92 and D94) were the most destabilizing. These destabilizing residues fall in a narrow higher-energy region of the energies. Analysis of the energy profile (Figure 2) shows two additional destabilizing residues, which do not directly interact with calcium ions (D61 and E100) in the most extended conformation), are sequentially and spatially close to the functional residues. Thus, the functional residues are located on short sequences of destabilizing residues. E108 is at the C-terminus and the terminal residues may often be destabilizing whether they are functional or not.

It is interesting to notice that the residues D51 and D53 were the most destabilizing in the tertiary structure but not in the most extended conformation. On the contrary, these two residues become stabilizing (dG<0), as follows from the comparison of the profile in Figure 2 and of the Figure 1a of the 1st part of this article. A similar feature was observed in APase (Tables 2,3) where H331 of the active site and an "adjacent" K127 were the most destabilizing in the 3D but became the most stabilizing in 2D calculations. Apparently, these differences between the 3D and 2D calculations indicate that the unfavorable packing in the tertiary structure makes these residues strongly destabilizing. The case of Apase, by the way, is also interesting from another point of view: although there were no common residues between 3D and 2D calculations, some of the known functional residues were still identified in 2D calculations.

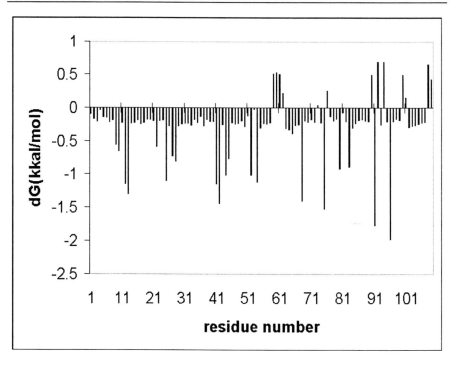

Figure 2. The energy profile for the most extended conformation of parvalbumin. Compare with the energy profile for the tertiary structure (Figure 1a of the 1st part of this article).

Even in such simple case as parvalbumin, one cannot generalize that sequence clusters of the charged residues of the same charge are always destabilizing. The sequence of parvalbumin, for example, contains clusters of the residues of positive charge (Figure 1a) and these residues are among the most stabilizing (Table 3), contrary to obvious expectation. At the same time, in CRO protein the clusters of the charged residues strongly are destabilizing. Then, a seemingly destabilizing pair of negatively charged residues D41-D42 (Table 3) is not destabilizing at all, again contrary to expectation. The relationship between the sequence clusters of the charged residues and the most destabilizing residues will be discussed further. Here it suffices to notice that a sequence pattern that would identify the functional residues from sequence (as the 2D calculations do) and with little percentage of the false positives (see Table 2) would be quite intricate. Moreover, such a sequence pattern is very likely to work only for a particular protein thus not having any value for prediction of the functional residues from sequence.

In barstar, all of the experimentally determined functional residues involved in the interaction with barnase (D33, D36, D40, E77 and E81) were destabilizing both in the tertiary and the most extended conformations. In both conformations, 4 out of 5 residues (excluding E76) were the top-most destabilizing. Calculations on the unfolded conformation have identified four destabilizing residues with no known function (E29, E47, E24 and E53). The residues E29 and E47 were within the region of the molecule involved in protein-protein interaction with the barnase.

It is also interesting to compare the energy profile/histogram obtained in calculations on the tertiary structure (parvalbumin, Figure 1a of the 1st part) and on the most extended conformation (Figure 2 of this, 2nd, part). Apart from the already mentioned D51 and D53, there are several other features distinguishing the diagrams obtained in 3D calculations (folded structure) from the diagrams obtained in 2D calculations (unfolded structure). Similar peculiarities are also characteristic a number of proteins in the set. The C-terminal residues were mildly stabilizing in the tertiary structure but became strongly destabilizing in the most extended conformation. Although the sequence regions of the most destabilizing and the most stabilizing residues are the same, the individual values of the per-residue energies can differ up to 50%. In particular, E62 was the most destabilizing in the tertiary (folded) structure but not the most destabilizing (though still destabilizing) in the most extended (unfolded) conformation. D76 is stabilizing in tertiary structure and destabilizing in the most extended conformation. Therefore, for this particular residue, the destabilizing contribution of the secondary structure is overcome by a greater stabilizing contribution of the tertiary packing. In short, a few of the residues do change significantly their energetical properties when protein folds into the tertiary structure. However, the general role of the tertiary structure seems to be rather a fine adjustment of the energies of the individual residues than an abrupt change in the energetical properties.

Functional and the Most Destabilizing Residues in an Additional Set of Proteins

Both the most destabilizing and the most stabilizing residues are likely to be functional in the tertiary (Tables 3&4 of the 1st part) as well as in the most extended conformation (Tables 2&3). However, the most destabilizing residues are more likely to be functional, especially in the tertiary structure. As it was mentioned above, in a number of proteins the most stabilizing residues have no known function (parvalbumin, FeSOD, cytochrome P450, calbindin, myoglobin, and barstar and CRO protein, Table 3). Using only the most destabilizing residues also allows to reduce the number of the false positives. Therefore, the method of identification of the most destabilizing residues using secondary structure (2D) was applied to another set of about 20 proteins. These proteins were of different biochemistry, tertiary folds (architecture) and size. The proteins were picked from PDB more or less randomly, only availability of the literature on the functional sites was taken into account. The proteins were of very diverse functions and included enzymes, proteins involved in various protein-protein interactions, ion channels, metal-, DNA-, sugar-binding, fatty acid binding and heme-binding proteins. The experimental secondary structure definitions derived from the PDB files were used in these predictions. Important functional residues were identified in all of the proteins: catalytic and substrate binding residues in enzymes, residues of the binding sites in the metal-, DNA- and sugar-binding proteins, and residues of the protein-protein interfaces. The results of the calculations are summarized in Table 4, the data for the ion channels are given in the Table 5. Some of the known functional residues were among the top 5% most destabilizing residues. There were relatively few false positives or residues of unknown function (Table 4). Often, there were other destabilizing residues close to the functional sites either in sequence (1-2 residues) or spatially (less than 6.0 angstrom). These features were also observed in the initial set of the proteins (Table 2) and in the spatial structure (Table 3 of the 1st part).

As in the case of the previously analyzed proteins (Table 2), many of the destabilizing residues are charged (Table 4). This is not surprising since charged residues are common in enzyme catalytic sites and in binding sites for polar ligands. However, hydrophobic and other non-polar residues were also predicted: in inter-subunit contacts and binding sites of hydrophobic ligands. Moreover, in fatty acid binding and heme-binding proteins most of the residues of the binding pockets are hydrophobic and the method directly identified at least some of the binding residues (Table 4). Some of the "adjacent" destabilizing residues were next in sequence to the known hydrophobic residues that actually comprise the binding pockets. For example, in the lipid-binding protein (1adl_), destabilizing K37, G26, K105 and D76 were next to the functional P38, V25, I104 and A75 forming the binding site.

The method was also found to be applicable to several ion channels (Table 5). The only difficulty was that at present it is not possible to distinguish between various types of the functional residues (those forming the pore, subunit-subunit contacts and sites for allosteric ligands). In the annexin xii hexamer (PDB 1aei), the center of the four domains has been proposed as the path of the voltage-gated ion channel and mutation [11] of one of the residues (E95, human, E92, *H.vulgaris*) in the central channel influences the channel function [12]. As the mutated E95, the most destabilizing E133 and E142 are also located in the central channel. The procedure also identifies residues involved in the protein –protein interactions forming the hexamer, some of the calcium-binding residues and a residue (R245) located in the central cavity of each monomer. This central cavity of a monomer is able to bind a small molecule ligand and is likely to be functionally important [13]. The CLC chloride channel (PDB 1kpl_A) is a homo-dimeric protein [14] with a pore in each subunit. Some residues of the dimer interface, residues inside the channel (F269 A396 E148) and the residues lining the pore (R126 R123 D278 E111) were identified. In MSCL (mechano-sensitive ion channel, PDB 1msl_A), most of the residues identified are involved in the protein-protein interactions forming the channel and most of these residues form the interface between each pair two consecutive chains of the pore. The identified residues of the channel comprise the so-called "occluded region of the pore" [15] (R98 K99 E104). K100, E102 of the occluded region were the most stabilizing residues, as well as G24 which is known to be important for gating [15].

Predictions from Amino Acid Sequence

At present, secondary structure can be predicted from amino acid sequence at an average accuracy of 80% [6][7][16]. Thus, it becomes possible to make an actual prediction of the functional residues using amino acid sequence as the only input. The secondary structure predictions for this purpose were obtained using Psi-pred [6]. The proteins analyzed were barstar, barnase, parvalbumin, CRO protein, APase, Ras protein and Snase. The average accuracy of the predictions (as measured by $Q3_{total}$ score [8]) was 85%. The energy histograms produced by the calculations on the most extended conformations using the predicted secondary structure showed only minor differences compared to the calculations using the experimentally derived secondary structure (as presented in the Tables 2&3). The average "efficiencies" of the predictions were 50% for known functional plus adjacent residues and 25% for known functional residues only. The corresponding averages for the PDB-derived secondary structures were not much higher: 55% and 25-30% (as shown in "total" row, Tables 2&3). Therefore, the method apparently can be used for prediction of the functional residues from amino acid sequence. The method was, actually, already applied to several yet not fully characterized proteins such as human oas1b and others [17][18] and the results appear to be compatible with the available though not yet published biochemical studies.

Sequence Clusters of the Charged Residues and the Functional Residues

Most of the proteins contained sequential clusters of charged residues and this fact was reflected in the results of the calculations of the most destabilizing residues. The basic physical assumption is that the charges of the same sign repulse. Therefore, it may seem to be quite apparent that several residues of the same charge clustered together close in sequence would make each other more destabilizing. In order to assess the relationship between the most destabilizing residues and the sequence clusters of the charged residues, the sequence clusters were defined here as "at least three residues of the same charge (D, E or R, K) spaced by no more than 2 residues". The respective sequence patterns for this rule can be written as [DE]-X(0,2)-[DE]-X(0,2)-[DE] or [RK]-X(0,2)-[RK]-X(0,2)-[RK]. The analysis shows that the clusters of charged residues were not always the top-most destabilizing. The tested set of proteins contains a total of 39 negative and 32 positive charged (Table 6) clusters but only 23 negative and 21 positive of these charge clusters were calculated to be the most destabilizing. Furthermore, 21 of the 23 negative and 16 of the 21 positive of the most destabilizing charged clusters indeed contained residues of the known functional sites. Only 2 negative and 5 positive charged clusters were calculated to be most destabilizing and were not associated with a known functional site. At least 7 proteins contained no charged clusters as defined (1b27_D, 2stl_E, 1ciq_A, 1isb_A, 2gbp_, 1daz_C, 1jaf_A) yet the functional residues were identified with a low rate of false positives. Also, it was observed that the number of the common residues between 3D and 2D calculations (see Table 1 and the beginning of the Results and Discussion) vary observably. Therefore, the sequence clusters of the charged residues are not the only factor in determining the destabilizing properties of the residues.

Apart from the proteins without the sequence clusters of the charged residues (Table 6), even in such simple case as parvalbumin one cannot generalize that residue clusters of the same charge are always destabilizing or always contain functional residues. Let's analyze in detail the sequence patterns of the charged residues in parvalbumin (Figure 1a). Short 2-residue clusters occur too often and were not analyzed in the Table 6. There are at least six of such short clusters in parvalbumin (using the pattern [DE]-X(0,3)-[DE]). However, only one of these six short clusters was identified as the most destabilizing (Table 1) and it contained the functional E101. Moreover, a seemingly destabilizing pair of negatively charged residues D41-D42 is not destabilizing either (though general considerations suggest that it should be). Actually, D41-D42 is among the most stabilizing (Table 3). There are also two 3-residue clusters of the type [DE]-X(0,2)-[DE]-X(0,2)-[DE] which contain the residues of the Ca-binding sites (Table 2) and two 3-residue clusters of the positive residues (26-28 HKK, 36-38 KKK and 44-48 KKvfH). None of these clusters was the most destabilizing or the most stabilizing, contrary to expectation (in general, residues of the same charge are in strongly repulsive interactions). Instead, among the most stabilizing were completely different positive residues (Table 3). At the same time, the clusters of the residues of positive charge are destabilizing in, for example, CRO protein and in other DNA-binding proteins. These and other intricacies of the sequence environment in only one protein of a relatively simple structure and function give a hint of the growing complexity of the sequence patterns that would be able to mimic reliably the results of the molecular mechanics calculations. Moreover, the charged residues are not the only typical types of the most destabilizing/stabilizing residues. Other residue types that were consistently identified as the most destabilizing were, for example, glycines and prolines (see Table 2). An approach of mimicking calculations with some sequence patterns would be complicated even further and will produce even more false positives as several kinds of patterns should be applied to a sequence.

Following this line of argument, it becomes clear that molecular mechanics provides more specific information than analysis of any putative sequence patterns made of the charged/gly/pro/etc residues. The molecular mechanics calculations apparently distinguish between the charged clusters in the sequence that are more likely to be functional. The calculations also identify as the most destabilizing residues which are not charged at all (though such residues are not very frequent). In other words, although sequence clusters of the charged residues are indeed an important factor, the presence of sequence clusters is hardly the only factor in determining the per-residue energies. The results suggest that relationship between relative energetical contributions of individual residues to stability and some kinds of explicit sequence patterns is far from being trivial.

Table 6. Sequence clusters of the charged residues, their destabilizing and functional properties. The PDB identifiers of the proteins are ordered alphabetically. The sequence clusters of charged residues were defined as [DE]-X(0,2)-[DE]-X(0,2)-[DE] or [RK]-X(0,2)-[RK]-X(0,2)-[RK]). Overlapping clusters (for example, "residues 7-9" and "residues 8-10") were counted as one ("residues 7-10"). Not all of the clusters were the most destabilizing. The majority of the identified clusters indeed contained functional residues. Some of the protein sequences (marked in gray) did not seem to contain any of the large charged clusters

Protein	D/E clusters	D/E destabilizing	D/E functional	R/K clusters	R/K destabilizing	R/K functional
1abf_	1	0	0	1	1	1
1adl_	2	1	1	2	2	2
1aei_A	4	2	2	1	1	1
1b07_A	3	1	1	1	0	0
1b27_A	0			1	1	1
1b27_D	0			0		
1bxi_A	4	3	3	0		
1cbw_D	0			2	2	2
1cc5_	1	1	0	0		
1ciq_A	0			0		
1daz_C	0			0		
1es7_A	1	1	1	1	1	0
1ew0_A	2	1	0	0		
1f8z_A	1	1	1	0		
1g5m_	1	0	0	1	0	0
1hel_	0			1	1	0
1hka_	0			1	1	0
1hmt_	1	1	1	1	1	1
1isb_A	0			0		
1jaf_A	0			0		
1jk8_A	3	2	1	1	1	1
1jk8_B	1	1	0	1	1	0
1kpl_A	1	1	1	2	1	1
1lfo_	1	1	1	3	1	1
1mdc_	1	0	0	1	1	1
1msl_A	0			1	0	0
1pmi_	3	0	0	2	0	0
1rtp_1	2	2	2	2	0	0
1run_A1	2	1	1	0		
1run_A2	0			1	0	0
1spd_A	2	1	1	0		

2gbp_	0			0		
2ifb_	1	1	1	3	3	3
2stl_E	0			0		
3cro_L	0			3	2	1
3icb_	1	1	1	0		
Total	39	23	21	32	21	16

"False Positives" among the Most Destabilizing and the Most Stabilizing Residues

Quite a number of the residues with the extremal energy values were neither known to be functional nor were anywhere around the main functional sites. Such residues were termed as "false positives" in this article. Strictly speaking, "false positive" is not entirely appropriate term as the method under consideration does not make any statistical generalizations but simply calculates energies of the individual residues. In other words, these "false positives" can be yet uncharacterized functional residues.

For example, a number of the proteins analyzed in this study were oligomeric. The role of oligomerization for the catalytic activity was reliably studied only for a few proteins with known structure (mostly, these were glycolytic proteins [19]). Still, it is known that the protein-protein contact, for example, in APase is essential for the catalytic activity of this enzyme [20]. "Adjacent" D53 in Cu-SOD is also located in the protein-protein interface of this dimeric enzyme. Adjacent K57 and "false positives" K69, P210 and A181 in LDH are forming the protein-protein interfaces of this tetrameric enzyme. Moreover, despite that the main oligomeric state of the APase is dimer; the enzyme can tetramerize [21], although biological significance of this tetramerization is not known. The "false positives" K312, D344, I346, R351 and K358 in APase (Tables 2&3) form the potential interface of the tetramer. These residues are located at the same region of the molecular surface as proposed in [21].

In a number of proteins, some of the "false positives" were involved in the formation of the "salt bridges" or ion-pairs. For example, the most stabilizing K202 and the most destabilizing D249 formed an ion-pair interaction in the tertiary structure of cellulase E2. In m-fabp, a salt bridge was formed between false positive K96 and E101. It should be noted that not less than 30% of the proteins analyzed in the set had among the "false positives" residues involved in formation of these ion-pairs.

It can also be observed (comparing the Tables 2&3) that the most stabilizing and the most stabilizing residues adjacent in the amino acid sequence are more likely to be functional. Such pairs occur in 40-50% of the proteins. On average over the set, approximately 28 of such pairs were known to be functional while only 15 of such pairs were not. In other words, the odds ratio for such a pattern to be functional is about 2.0 (P<0.01). Therefore, presence of such a residue pattern suggests that at least one of the residues of the pair is 2 times more likely to be functional than not. Absence of such pairs, however, does not indicate that all of the residues identified in a protein are non-functional.

The most apparent method to find the more important residues among the most destabilizing and the most stabilizing residues is to use the data on sequence similarity. However, as it was already mentioned in the 1st part of this study, 1. The sequence data might be not always available and 2. Absence of the sequence similarity in no way suggests absence of the function of the residue. Another approach is spatial clustering. In the case of calculations on the tertiary (spatial) structure false positives, as it was shown in the 1st part of this study, can be easily eliminated by using the spatial clustering of the residues. Although such clustering inevitably eliminates a number of actually functional residues, it is an effective way to identify the main functional site in the tertiary structure. In the case of the calculations on the most extended conformation such an alternative is not available. However, sequence clustering can be used instead. In brief, first we map all of the most destabilizing and the most stabilizing residues in, for example, barstar protein on the sequence (see Tables 2, 3). Then, the few sequence regions of about 10-residue long that contain the maximal numbers of the most destabilizing/stabilizing residues would be the regions of the actual functional site (compare with the data for barstar in the Table 1 of the 1st part).

Even more practical approach to reduce false positives would be using some additional biochemical information. For example, let's use the following piece of biochemical information: calbindin is a calcium-binding protein. It should be noticed that the roles of the positively-charged residues in the calcium-binding sites of the protein are yet to be established. In particular, the positively charged residues in the immediate vicinity of the Ca-binding sites of the calbindin can stabilize the protein's structure by holding together the negatively-charged clusters of the Ca-binding site itself. However, it is clear that the most important functional residues are very likely to be negatively charged (as Ca-ion is positively charged). This piece of information automatically removes all of the positively charged residues as false positives (Table 3). Another example: CRO-protein is a DNA-binding protein. Generally, DNA-binding residues are much more likely to be positively charged (to interact effectively with the negatively charged phosphates of the nucleic backbone). And yet another example: the results for fatty-acid binding proteins show that there are typically 4-6 destabilizing residues immediately adjacent to the residues forming the hydrophobic binding pocket. Thus, if the protein is likely to form a hydrophobic binding site (as in the case of fatty acid and hem-binding proteins), then almost 3/4 of the residues that form the hydrophobic binding pockets can be identified by taking the hydrophobic residues next in sequence to the most destabilizing residues. Although applying such bits of information as rules will exclude a number of actually functional residues (see Tables 2&3 for calbindin, CRO protein and fab proteins), these examples show that the results of the calculations can be interpreted and adjusted using a minimal biochemical information (such as what is the most basic function of the protein in question: metal- or DNA-binding etc).

Modeling Random Conformations with the Same Secondary Structure

It is quite clear (from the results presented above as well as from using the basic physical sense) that the most extended conformation is the best choice to model the effects of the secondary structure on the energetical differences between individual residues. To demonstrate this, the choice of the linear extended conformation was additionally assessed by identifying destabilizing residues in 10 randomly built unfolded conformations with the secondary structure of the native protein. These random structures were more compact than the most extended conformation but lacked any organized tertiary structure. Some examples of these random conformations are shown in the Figure 3. Similar observations were made for parvalbumin, barstar, barnase, CuSOD, Cro-protein and SH3 domain. Generally, the functional residues were the top-most destabilizing in the most extended conformation (Figure 1a) but not in the random unfolded conformations. For example, in parvalbumin, residues E59, E62, D94 and E101 of the Ca-binding sites (Table 1, Figure 2a) were destabilizing (dG>0) in 9 out of 10 random conformations. However, these residues were not the most destabilizing but were located in the middle regions of the energy histograms. The residues D90 and D92 were identified only in 5 of the 10 random models. Thus, the model of the most extended conformation identifies the known functional residues more reliably than a random unfolded model with the same secondary

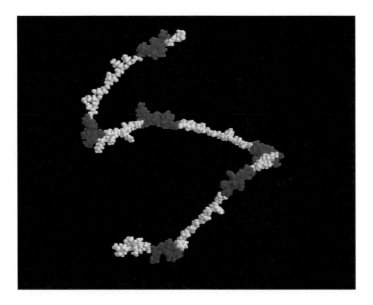

Figure 3a

Figure 3b

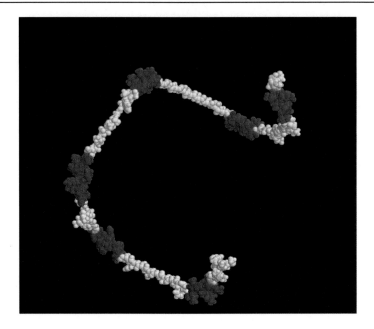

Figure 3c

Figure 3. Random semi-compact conformations with the same secondary structure as the most extended conformation, on the example of parvalbumin. The most extended conformation is shown in the Figure 1d. a)-c) Random semi-compact conformations.

structure. Nevertheless, the results show that the destabilizing residues still are destabilizing even in random conformations of the same secondary structure through a statistical analysis of such conformations.

Secondary Structure, Protein Folding and the Functional Residues

Several considerations further support the physical and biological validity of the method under consideration. Firstly, a strong correlation between the secondary structure contents and the protein architecture [22] suggests that the tertiary structure (and, therefore, the protein function) may to a large extent be influenced by the secondary structure alone. The present study shows that the extent of this influence could be about 40%, on average. Secondly, the functional residues are often placed in cavities and thus have relatively high surface accessibility instead of being densely packed in the protein interior. Therefore, the destabilizing effect of the functional residues is likely to act mostly at the level of the secondary structure. Indeed, comparison of the 3D/2D energy profiles (presented above) shows that the formation of the tertiary structure mostly leads to the fine adjustments of the per-residue energies (with the exception of a few residues). Thirdly, the electrostatic effects can be particularly important in determining the energetic differences between the residues [23]. Apart from the basic physics, long-range (12-15 Å) electrostatic effects on function were actually experimentally observed in proteins. Therefore, even in a significantly extended conformation of a protein, the electrostatic field of one residue may involve interactions with at least 10-20 sequentially arranged residues (depending on the exact types of the secondary structure elements). These long range interactions depend on the secondary structure and the unique amino acid sequence and thus explain the difficulty of mimicking the results of the energy calculations using the sequence patterns, as it was shown above.

Fourthly and finally, the solved ribosome structure [24] directly suggests that any protein is likely to assume the most extended conformation immediately after the ribosomal synthesis. An extended conformation, which is a linear arrangement of the secondary structure elements with no tertiary organization, is consistent with the elongated narrow channel observed in the ribosome structure [24]. Such a channel can accommodate only an extended protein structure not wider than an alpha-helix, beta-strand or loop. Actually, the secondary structure is not a mere abstraction or classification but rather a definite step in the physical process of the protein folding [4]. The amino acid sequence outlines the secondary structure and determines folding of the protein in a number of other ways. After the secondary structure (Figure 1b) is formed, the individual energetical differences between the residues are more distinct than in a completely unfolded sequence (Figure 1a). Then these differences are further clarified and finely adjusted in the fully folded (tertiary) structure (Figure 1c) by means of the tertiary packing of the side-chains. Thus, the concept of the most extended conformation (Figure 1d), central to the present study, is very likely to be a legitimate step in the cellular protein folding and not simply a theoretical approach to calculate the energetical effects of the secondary structure.

Conclusions

The results of the present study show that a number of the functional residues can be identified from sequence alone. The methodology is based on a structural model that is likely to represent protein conformation after ribosomal synthesis as well as on a molecular mechanics computation. The results emphasize the importance of the secondary structure for function and stability of proteins, and suggest that the functional residues have distinct energetic properties, even in a significantly unfolded state of a protein. Comparison of the energy profiles for the native and the most extended conformation also can distinguish between the residues that destabilize mostly tertiary structure (for example, D51, D53 in parvalbumin) and those destabilizing the secondary structure. This kind of analysis may be important for protein engineering. There is still the difficulty of distinguishing between the various types of the functional residues and the "false positives". Consequently, a number of approaches to interpret the results of the calculations were proposed. Nevertheless, the predicted residues include enzyme catalytic and substrate binding residues, residues that bind metal ions, DNA and sugars, residues of various protein-protein interfaces and of the pores of ion channels. As the functional residues are the biophysical basis of the biological activity of any protein, the method has a wide range of potential applications in deciphering and annotation of the human and other genomes, rational protein engineering and, in perspective, for the discovery of the novel genetic markers for the phenotype-genotype studies and medical diagnostics.

Acknowledgements

I would like to thank Prof. Yu V Torshin for his invaluable support and the advice in writing this article.

References

[1]   http://www.functionalgenomics.org.uk/sections/programme/index.htm
[2]   Kelley, L.A., MacCallum, R.M.& Sternberg, M.J. (2000) *J. Mol. Biol.* 299, 499-520.
[3]   Hulo N, Sigrist CJ, Le Saux V, Langendijk-Genevaux PS, Bordoli L, Gattiker A, De Castro E, Bucher P, Bairoch A. *Nucleic Acids Res.* 2004 Jan 1;32 Database issue: D134-7.
[4]   Torshin IY, Harrison RW. Protein folding: search for basic physical models. *ScientificWorldJournal.* 2003 Jul 30;3:623-35. Review.
[5]   Frishman, D. & Argos, P. (1995) *Proteins* 23, 566-579.
[6]   Jones, D. T. (1999) *J. Mol. Biol.* 292, 195-202.

[7] Kilosanidze, G. T., Kutsenko, A. S., Esipova, N. G. & Tumanyan, V. G. (2002) *FEBS Lett.* 510, 13-16.

[8] Schulz, G. E. & Schirmer, R. H. (1979) *Principles of Protein Structure.* Ed. Cantor, C. R. (Springer-Verlag, New York), pp 125-126.

[9] Abagyan, R.A., Totrov, M.M. and Kuznetsov, D.N. (1994). *J.Comp.Chem.* 15, 488-506.

[10] McPhalen, C. A., Sielecki, A. R., Santarsiero, B. D. & James, M. N. (1994) *J. Mol. Biol.* 235, 718-732.

[11] H. Luecke, B.T. Chang,W.S.Maillliard,D.D. Schlaepfer, H.T. Haigler. *Nature* 378, 512 (1995)

[12] R. Berendes, D. Voges, P. Demange, R. Huber, A. Burger. *Science* 262(5132):427-30 (1993)

[13] N.Kaneko, H. Ago, R.Matsuda, E. Inagaki, M. Miyano *J. Mol Biol.* 274,16 (1997)

[14] R. Dutzler, E.B. Campbell, M. Cadene, B.T. Chait, R. MacKinnon. *Nature* 415,287 (2002)

[15] Chang, R.H. Spencer, A.T. Lee, M.T. Barclay, D.C. Rees *Science* 282, 2220 (1998)

[16] Lattman, E. E. (2001) *Proteins* 45 Suppl 5, 1-2.

[17] Torshin IY. *Functional residues- from amino acid sequence.* SERMACS 2003:55th Southeast Regional Meeting of the American Chemical Society, 2003, Atlanta, GA, USA A164

[18] Torshin IY. *Computed energetics of macromolecules: identification of the functional residues in proteins and functional nucleotides in RNA.* 227th meeting of American Chemical Society, Division of physical chemistry, March 28 2004, Anaheim, CA, USA, A345

[19] Torshin IY. *Med Sci Monit.* 2002 Apr;8(4):BR123-35.

[20] Kim EE, Wyckoff HW. *J Mol Biol.* 1991 Mar 20;218(2):449-64.

[21] Chaplin, M.F., Torshin, I.Y., Poltorak, O.M., Chukhray, E.S., Atyaksheva, L.F., Trevan, M.D. *J Mol Cat B ,* 7(1-4):165-172 1999

[22] Li, Q. Z. & Lu, Z. Q. (2001) *J. Theor. Biol.* 213, 493-502.

[23] Elcock, A. H. (2001) *J. Mol. Biol.* 312, 885-96.

[24] Nissen, P., Hansen, J., Ban, N., Moore, P. B. & Steitz, T. A. (2000) *Science* 289, 920-930.

[25] G. Parkinson et al., *Nat. Struct. Biol.* 3(10), 837 (1996).

[26] C. Kleanthous et al., *Nat. Struct. Biol.* 6(3), 243 (1999).

[27] Carter DC, Melis KA, O'Donnell SE, Burgess BK, Furey WR Jr, Wang BC, Stout CD. *J Mol Biol.* 1985 Jul 20;184(2):279-95.

[28] Archer, M., Banci, L., Dikaya, E., Romao, M. J.. *J Biol Inorg Chem* 2 pp. 611 (1997)

[29] Petros, A. M., Medek, A., Nettesheim, D. G., Kim, D. H., Yoon, H. S., Swift, K., Matayoshi, E. D., Oltersdorf, T., Fesik, S. W. *Proc.Nat.Acad.Sci.USA* 98 pp. 3012 (2001)

[30] R. Bott et al., *J. Biol. Chem.* 263(16), 7895 (1988).

[31] J. L. Neira et al., *Fold. Des.* 1(3), 189 (1996).

[32] G. L. Shaw, B. Davis, J. Keeler, A. R. Fersht, Biochemistry. 34(7), 2225 (1995).

[33] Miyatake, H., Kanai, M., Adachi, S., Nakamura, H., Tamura, K., Tanida, H., Tsuchiya, T., Iizuka, T., Shiro, Y. *Acta Crystallogr., Sect.D* 55 pp. 1215 (1999)

[34] K. P. Wilson, B. A. Malcolm, B. W. Matthews, *J. Biol. Chem.* 267(15), 10842 (1992).

[35] B. Xiao, G. Shi, X. Chen, H. Yan, X. Ji, *Structure. Fold. Des.* 7(5), 489 (1999).

[36] Thompson, J., Winter, N., Terwey, D., Bratt, J., Banaszak, L. *J Biol Chem* 272 pp. 7140 (1997)

[37] N. K. Vyas, M. N. Vyas, F. A. Quiocho, *Science.* 242(4883), 1290 (1988).

[38] Clayton, D. J., Brereton, I. M., Kroon, P. A., Smith, R. *FEBS Lett.* 479 pp. 118 (2000)

[39] A. J. Scheidig, T. R. Hynes, L. A. Pelletier, J. A. Wells, A. A. Kossiakoff, *Protein. Sci.* 6(9), 1806 (1997).

[40] J. T. Nguyen, C. W. Turck, F. E. Cohen, R. N. Zuckermann, W. A. Lim, *Science.* 282(5396), 2088 (1998).

[41] B. Mahalingam et al., *Eur. J. Biochem.* 263(1), 238 (1999).

[42] T. Kirsch, W. Sebald, M. K. Dreyer, *Nat. Struct. Biol.* 7(6), 492 (2000).

[43] Benning, M. M., Smith, A. F., Wells, M. A., Holden, H. M. *J Mol Biol* 228 pp. 208 (1992)

[44] LaLonde, J. M., Levenson, M. A., Roe, J. J., Bernlohr, D. A., Banaszak, L. J. *J Biol Chem* 269 pp. 25339 (1994)

In: Trends in Bioinformatics Research
Editor: Peter V. Yan, pp. 33-57

ISBN 1-59454-739-4
© 2005 Nova Science Publishers, Inc.

Chapter II

Family Classification and Integrative Analysis for Protein Functional Annotation

Cathy H. Wu[1], Hongzhan Huang[1], Anastasia Nikolaskaya[1], C. R. Vinayaka[2], Sehee Chung[1] and Jian Zhang[2]

[1]Department of Biochemistry and Molecular Biology and
[2]National Biomedical Research Foundation,
Georgetown University Medical Center, Washington, DC, USA

Abstract

The high-throughput genome projects have resulted in a rapid accumulation of predicted protein sequences, however, experimentally-verified information on protein function lags far behind. The common approach to inferring function of uncharacterized proteins based on sequence similarity to annotated proteins in sequence databases often results in over-identification, under-identification, or even misannotation. To facilitate accurate, consistent and rich functional annotation of proteins, PIR employs a classification-driven rule-based automated annotation method supported by a bioinformatics framework that provides data integration and associative analysis. The PIRSF classification system provides protein classification from superfamily to subfamily levels in a network structure to reflect evolutionary relationship of full-length proteins, including the preservation of domain architecture. Family-specific rules are manually defined to allow for conditional propagation of such annotation as functional site residues and protein names from characterized proteins to unknown proteins. The iProClass integration of protein family, function and structure data allows associative analyses of proteins. The integrative approach leads to novel prediction and functional inference for uncharacterized proteins, allows systematic detection of genome annotation errors, and provides sensible propagation and standardization of protein annotation.

Keywords: data integration, family classification, PIR (Protein Information Resource), PIRSF family, protein annotation, protein family, protein function, rule-base, UniProt

1. Introduction

The high-throughput genome projects have resulted in a rapid accumulation of predicted protein sequences for a large number of organisms. Meanwhile, scientists have begun to tackle protein functions and other complex regulatory processes using global-scale data generated at various levels of biological organization, ranging from genomes and proteomes to metabolomes and physiomes. To fully realize the value of the data, scientists need to understand how these proteins function in making up a living cell. With experimentally-verified information on protein function lagging behind, bioinformatics methods are needed for reliable and large-scale functional annotation of proteins.

A general approach for functional annotation of unknown proteins is to infer protein functions based on sequence similarity to annotated proteins in sequence databases. While this is a powerful method, numerous genome annotation errors have been detected, many of which have been propagated throughout molecular databases. There are several sources of errors (Galperin and Koonin, 1998; Koonin and Galperin, 2003). Errors often occur when identification is made based on local domain similarity or similarity involving only parts of the query and target molecules. (A comparison of two proteins can yield a high score either because they share one common domain of very high similarity or because they have consistent moderate similarity over the entire lengths of the proteins. Many identification errors have occurred because of the failure to distinguish these cases.) Furthermore, the similarity may be to a known domain that is tangential to the main function of the protein or to a region with compositional similarity, such as transmembrane domains. Errors also occur when the best hit entry is an uncharacterized or poorly annotated protein, or is itself incorrectly predicted, or simply has a different function. Aside from erroneous annotation, database entries may be under-identified, such as a "hypothetical protein" with a convincing similarity to a protein or domain of known function, and may be over-identified, such as ascribing a specific enzyme activity when a less specific one would be more appropriate.

The Protein Information Resource (PIR) (Wu *et al.*, 2003a) is a public bioinformatics resource that supports comparative analysis and functional annotation of proteins. The PIR-International Protein Sequence Database of functionally annotated protein sequences grew out of the *Atlas of Protein Sequence and Structure* edited by Margaret Dayhoff (1965-1978). The previously independent protein sequence database activities of PIR, the European Bioinformatics Institute, and the Swiss Institute of Bioinformatics are now joined to establish UniProt—the Universal Protein Resource—a central resource of protein sequence and function that unifies PIR-PSD, Swiss-Prot, and TrEMBL (Apweiler *et al.*, 2004).

For accurate and comprehensive annotation, PIR uses a classification-driven rule-based annotation method, which first classifies query proteins into curated protein families, then applies rules tailored specifically to individual protein families. Family-specific rules would define not only the conditions that must be met, but also the fields that could be propagated. Furthermore, use of non-sequence-based "associative analyses" can provide additional information to enhance functional annotation of proteins.

2. PIR Protein Family Classification

Protein family classification provides effective means for large-scale genome annotation and biological knowledge discovery based on the information embedded within families of homologous sequences and their structures. The classification approach has several advantages. It improves detection of distantly related proteins that may not be evident in pairwise alignments; facilitates sensible propagation and standardization of protein annotation; allows systematic identification of annotation errors; assists the extraction of relevant biological information from vast amounts of data; provides valuable clues to structure, activity, and metabolic role; and reflects the underlying gene families, the analysis of which is essential for comparative genomics and phylogenomics.

There exist many protein classification databases. The classification may be based on protein structure (e.g., SCOP (Andreeva *et al.*, 2004)), function (e.g., Enzyme Nomenclature), or sequence (e.g., Pfam (Bateman *et al.*, 2004) and

PIRSF (Wu *et al.*, 2004a)). It may be based on domain (e.g., SCOP and Pfam), sequence motif (e.g., Prosite (Hulo *et al.*, 2004)), or full-length protein (e.g., PIRSF). While each of these databases is useful for particular needs, a full understanding of protein structure, function and evolutionary relationships require the integration and complementation of the various classification schemes.

2.1. PIRSF Classification Concept

The PIRSF (SuperFamily) classification system uses a network structure with multiple levels of sequence diversity from superfamilies to subfamilies to reflect evolutionary relationship of full-length proteins (Figure 1). Basing classification on full-length proteins allows annotation of biological functions, biochemical activities, and sequence features that are family specific. In contrast, the domain architecture of a protein provides insight into general functional and structural properties, as well as into complex evolutionary mechanisms. PIRSF classification, which considers both full-length similarity and domain architecture, discriminates between single- and multi-domain proteins where functional differences are associated with the presence or absence of one or more domains. Furthermore, classification based on whole proteins, rather than on the component domains, allows annotation of both generic biochemical and specific biological functions.

The primary PIRSF classification unit is the *homeomorphic family* whose members are both *homologous* (evolved from a common ancestor) and *homeomorphic* (sharing full-length sequence similarity and a common domain architecture). Each protein can be assigned to only one homeomorphic family, which may have zero or more parent *superfamilies* and zero or more child *subfamilies*. The parent superfamilies connect related families and orphan proteins based on one or more common domains, which may or may not extend over the entire lengths of the proteins. The child subfamilies are homeomorphic groups that may represent functional specialization. The flexible number of parent-child levels from superfamily to subfamily reflects natural clusters of proteins with varying degrees of sequence conservation. While a protein will belong to one and only one homeomorphic family, multi-domain proteins may belong to multiple superfamilies. A domain superfamily, which consists of all proteins that contain a particular domain, is usually represented by the corresponding Pfam domain for convenience.

Domain Superfamily • One common Pfam domain	PIRSF Superfamily • 0 or more levels • One or more common domains	PIRSF Homeomorphic Family • Exactly one level • Full-length sequence similarity and common domain architecture	PIRSF Homeomorphic Subfamily • 0 or more levels • Functional specialization
PF02735: Ku70/Ku80 beta-barrel domain	PIRSF800001: Ku70/80 autoantigen	PIRSF003033: Ku70 autoantigen PIRSF016570: Ku80 autoantigen	
		PIRSF006493: Ku, prokaryotic type	
PF00219: Insulin-like growth factor binding protein (IGFBP)		PIRSF001969: IGFBP	PIRSF500001: IGFBP-1 ... PIRSF500006: IGFBP-6
		PIRSF018239: IGFBP-related protein, MAC25 type	
PF01817: Chorismate mutase (CM)		PIRSF017318: CM of AroQ class, eukaryotic type PIRSF001501: CM of AroQ class, prokaryotic type PIRSF026640: Periplasmic CM PIRSF001500: Bifunctional CM/PDT (P-protein) PIRSF001499: Bifunctional CM/PDH (T-protein)	
PF02153: Prephenate dehydrogenase (PDH)		PIRSF001499: Bifunctional CM/PDH (T-protein) PIRSF006786: PDH, feedback inhibition-insensitive PIRSF005547: PDH, feedback inhibition-sensitive	

Figure 1. PIRSF classification system based on evolutionary relationship of full-length proteins

2.2. PIRSF Examples

Figure 1 illustrates three PIRSF examples, one with a superfamily (PIRSF800001: Ku70/80 autoantigen), one with subfamilies (PIRSF001969: insulin-like growth factor binding protein, IGFBP), and one with multiple domain parents (PIRSF001499: bifunctional chorismate mutase/prephenate dehydrogenase, T-protein).

Ku is a multifunctional protein found in both eukaryotes and prokaryotes. The eukaryotic Ku protein is an obligate heterodimer of two subunits, Ku70 and Ku80.

Ku70 and Ku80, predicted to have evolved by gene duplication from a homodimeric ancestor, share three domains and are placed into one superfamily. They differ, however, at their carboxyl ends, so they form two homeomorphic families (PIRSF003033 and PIRSF016570). The central Ku beta-barrel domain (PF02735) is also conserved (without the N- and C-terminal extensions) in several prokaryotes (PIRSF006493). The prokaryotic Ku was predicted (Aravind and Koonin, 2001), and later experimentally confirmed, to form a homodimer involved in repairing double-strand breaks in DNA in a mechanistically similar fashion to eukaryotic Ku-containing proteins.

Insulin-like growth factor binding proteins (IGFBPs) are a group of vertebrate secreted proteins that bind to IGF with high affinity and modulate the biological actions of IGFs. These proteins share a common domain architecture, with an N-terminal IGF binding protein domain (PF00219) and a C-terminal thyroglobulin type-1 repeat domain, and are classified into a homeomorphic family (PIRSF001969). These proteins, however, have a highly variable mid-region and diverse functions ranging from the traditional IGF-related role to acting as growth factors independent of the IGFs. Six member types, IGFBP-1 through 6, have been delineated based on gene organization, sequence similarity, and binding affinity to IGFs (Baxter *et al.*, 1998). Each of the member types corresponds to a clearly distinguishable clade of the family phylogenetic tree and consists of orthologous sequences from various vertebrate species. Accordingly, six homeomorphic subfamilies (PIRSF500001-500006) are defined. The IGFBP family is related to the MAC25 gene family (PIRSF018239), which shares only the N-terminal IGFBP domain and has a relatively low IGF-binding activity.

Chorismate mutase (CM) (EC 5.4.99.5) and prephenate dehydrogenase (PDH) (EC 1.3.1.12) are two enzymes of the shikimate pathway present in bacteria, archaea, fungi, and plants. The corresponding domains (PF01817, PF02153) occur in proteins with different domain architectures, reflecting extensive domain shuffling. These proteins are classified into several PIRSF homeomorphic families according to their domain architectures and are assigned family names indicative of their known or predicted functions.

3. PIR Rule-Based Automated Annotation

The PIRSF classification serves as the basis for a rule-based approach that provides standardized and rich automatic functional annotation (Wu *et al.*, 2003b). In particular, annotation can be reliably propagated from sequences containing experimentally determined properties to closely related homologous sequences based on curated PIRSF families. PIR rules are manually defined and curated for several annotation fields, focusing specifically on position-specific sequence features, protein names, Enzyme Commission (EC) name and number, keywords, and Gene Ontology (GO) (Harris *et al.*, 2004) terms.

3.1. Position-Specific Site Rules

Position-specific site rules are developed for annotating active site residues, binding site residues, modified residues, or other functionally important amino acid residues. To exploit known structure information, site rules are defined starting with PIRSF families that contain at least one known 3D structure with experimentally-verified site information. The active site information on proteins is taken from the PDB (Bourne *et al.*, 2004) SITE records, the LIGPLOT of interactions available in PDBSum database (Laskowski, 2001), and published scientific literature. The Catalytic Site Atlas (CSA) (Porter *et al.*, 2004), a database documenting active sites and catalytic residues in enzymes of 3D structure, is used as an authoritative source for catalytic residues in enzyme active sites.

Rule Definition and Curation

The rules are defined using appropriate syntax and controlled vocabulary for site description and evidence attribution. As shown in Table 1, each rule consists of the rule ID, template sequence (a representative sequence with known 3D structure), rule condition, feature for propagation (denoting site feature to be propagated if the entire rule condition is tested true), and reference. The rules are PIRSF-specific and there may be more than one site rules for a PIRSF family. Accordingly, the rule ID is named based on PIRSF ID (e.g., PIRSR000125 for PIRSF000125), and suffixed with consecutive rule numbers within the PIRSF. Site rule curation involves manually editing multiple sequence alignment of representative PIRSF members (including the template PDB entry), visualizing site residues in the 3D structure, and building hidden Markov models (Eddy,

1998) for the conserved regions containing the functional site residues (referred to as "site HMMs"). The profile HMM thus built allows one to map functionally important residues from the template structure to other members of the PIRSF family which do not have a solved structure.

Rule Propagation

For site feature propagation, the entire rule condition is checked, which generally involves PIRSF membership checking, site HMM matching, and site residue matching. To avoid false positives, site features are only propagated automatically if all site residues match perfectly in the conserved region by aligning both the template and query sequences to the profile HMM using HmmAlign. Potential functional sites missing one or more residues or containing conservative substitutions are only annotated after expert review with evidence attribution. For accurate site propagation, sometimes it is necessary to match more residues in the rule condition than those to be propagated. For example, a total of eight catalytic and binding residues in sulfite reductase need to be matched in order to propagate the siroheme-ion binding residue (Cys) correctly (PIRSR000259-3, Table 1).

Evidence Attribution

Associated with the rule-based automated annotation is evidence tagging that distinguishes experimentally-verified from computationally-predicted annotation (Wu *et al.*, 2003b). In the new UniProt evidence attribution system, all protein annotation will be attributed for the data source, the types of evidence and methods for annotation (Apweiler *et al.*, 2004). Automatic annotation generated by the PIR rules will be attributed with the rule ID, with a link to the rule report where additional information will be displayed. The site rule report, directly accessible based on the rule ID, consists of rule definition, multiple sequence alignment (Figure 2A), and propagation status of each protein entry with detail results on HMM site match and HmmAlign residue match (Figure 2B). Such evidence attribution provides an effective means to avoid misinterpretation of annotation information and propagation of annotation errors.

3.2. Protein Name Rules

Protein name rules are defined for assigning standardized names to members of curated PIRSF families. The curated families, each with a unique ID and family

Table 1. PIR site rules for automated annotation of functional sites

Rule ID	Template ID	Rule Condition	Feature for Propagation	Reference
PIRSR0 00259-1	UniProt:P17846 PDB:1AOP	PIRSF000259 member Site match: Arg 82, Arg 152, Lys 214, Lys 216, Cys 433, Cys 439, Cys 478, Cys 482	ACT_SITE (Catalytic residues): Arg 82, Arg 152, Lys 214, Lys 216, Cys 482	CSA:1AOP PMID:93158 48, 9315849
PIRSR0 00259-2	UniProt:P17846 PDB:1AOP	PIRSF000259 member Site match: Arg 82, Arg 152, Lys 214, Lys 216, Cys 433, Cys 439, Cys 478, Cys 482	BINDING (4Fe-4S cluster): Cys 433, Cys 439, Cys 478, Cys 482	PMID:75699 52
PIRSR0 00259-3	UniProt:P17846 PDB:1AOP	PIRSF000259 member Site match: Arg 82, Arg 152, Lys 214, Lys 216, Cys 433, Cys 439, Cys 478, Cys 482	BINDING (Siroheme iron): Cys 482	PMID:75699 52
PIRSR0 00532-1	UniProt:P06998 PDB: 1PFK	PIRSF000532 member Site match: Gly 12, Arg 73, Thr 126, Asp 128, Arg 172	ACT_SITE (Catalytic residues): Gly 12, Arg 73, Thr 126, Asp 128, Arg 172	CSA:1PFK PMID: 2975709
PIRSR0 00532-2	UniProt:P06998 PDB: 1PFK	PIRSF000532 member Site match: Arg 163, Arg 244, His 250, Arg 253	BINDING (Fructose-1,6-Bisphosphate): Arg 163, Arg 244, His 250, Arg 253	PMID: 2975709
PIRSR0 00532-3	UniProt:P06998 PDB: 1PFK	PIRSF000532 member Site match: Glu 188	METAL (Magnesium): Glu 188	PMID: 2975709

name, are labeled with an evidence tag of "validated" to indicate those containing at least one member with experimentally-validated function, "predicted" for families whose functions are inferred computationally based on sequence similarity and/or functional associative analysis, or "tentative" to indicate cases where experimental evidence is not decisive. As with the site rule, each name rule is defined with conditions for propagation. While most name rules assign protein names to all family members, many families require more specialized rules with additional conditions to propagate appropriate names and avoid the over-identification or under-identification problem. Examples of specialized conditions include the presence of absence of functional sites or motifs, certain taxonomic lineage, and exceptions list. In addition to standardized protein names, the name

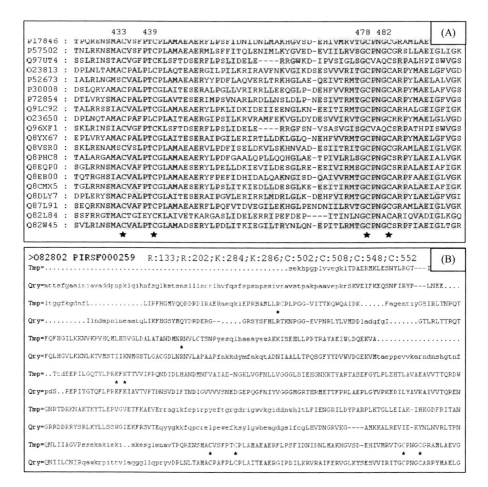

Figure 2. PIR site rule report for evidence attribution of rule-based feature propagation (see complete report at http://pir.georgetown.edu/cgi-bin/pirsiterule.pl?list=PIRSR000259-1) (A) Multiple sequence alignment of conserved regions containing functional sites (site residues are marked and numbered based on template sequence—P17846) (B) HMM profile alignment of query and template sequences (site residues are marked and numbered based on query sequence—O82802)

rules may also specify synonyms, acronyms or abbreviations, EC name and number, keywords and GO terms. For protein families containing commonly misannotated proteins, a "misnomer" field is added. The name rules will link to the underlying PIRSF report for evidence attribution (section 4.1, Figure 3).

4. iProClass Data Integration and Associative Analysis

Functional annotation for poorly characterized or unknown proteins may also require analysis and inference based on properties beyond sequence similarity. Factors that may be relevant include similarity of three-dimensional structures, metabolic capacities of the organisms, and evolutionary history of the protein as deduced from aligned sequences. In addition, protein function can be inferred using *associative analysis* ("guilt-by-association") based on system biology properties even when there is no detectable sequence similarity (Marcotte *et al.*, 1999; Koonin and Galperin, 2003; Osterman and Overbeek, 2003). Associative properties that have been demonstrated to allow inference of function not evident from sequence homology include: co-occurrence of proteins in operons or genome context (Overbeek *et al.*, 1999); proteins sharing common domains in fusion proteins; proteins in the same pathway, subcellular network or complex; proteins with correlated gene or protein expression patterns; and protein families with correlated taxonomic distribution (common phylogenetic/phyletic patterns) (Pellegrini *et al.*, 1999; Morett *et al.*, 2003).

4.1. iProClass Integrated Database

The iProClass database, designed to offer an integrated view of protein information (Huang *et al.*, 2003), serves as a bioinformatics framework for data integration and associative analysis of proteins (Wu *et al.*, 2004b). Containing comprehensive descriptions of proteins with up-to-date information from many sources, iProClass provides value-added views for all UniProt proteins and PIRSF protein families with extensive annotation and graphical display. Rich links to over 80 molecular databases are provided with source attribution, hypertext links, and related summary information extracted from the underlying sources, including databases of protein sequence, family, function, pathway, protein-protein interaction, post-translational modification, structure, genome, ontology, literature, and taxonomy. The source attribution and hypertext links facilitate exploration of additional information and examination of discrepant annotations from different sources.

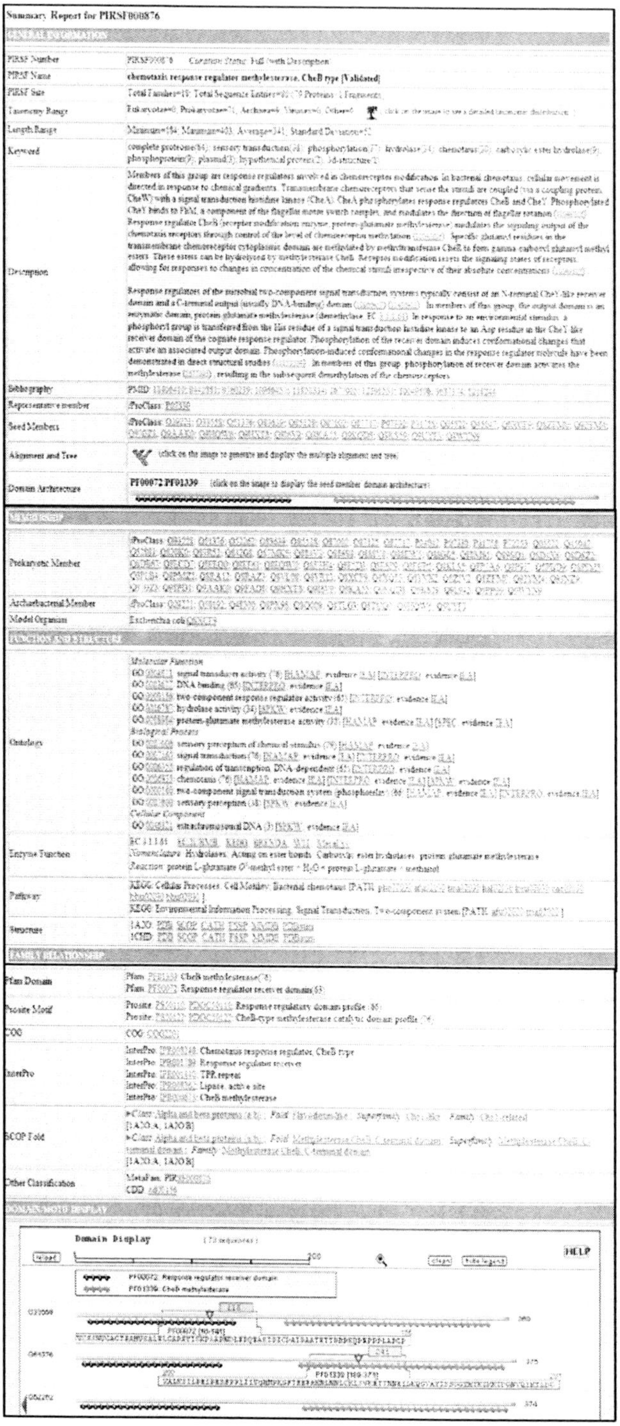

Figure 3. iProClass protein family report (This report, for the "chemotaxis response regulator methylesterase, CheB type" PIRSF family, can be viewed directly at http://pir.georgetown.edu/cgi-bin/ipcSF?id=SF000876)

iProClass presents value-added views for UniProt proteins and PIRSF protein families in protein and family summary reports, respectively. The protein summary report contains information on:

- General information: protein ID and name (with synonyms, alternative names), source organism taxonomy (with NCBI taxonomy ID, group, and lineage), and sequence annotations (such as gene names, keywords, function, and complex);
- Database cross-references: bibliography (with PubMed ID and link to a bibliography information and submission page), gene and genome databases, gene ontology (with GO hierarchy and evidence tag), enzyme/function (with EC hierarchy, nomenclature and reaction), pathway (with KEGG (Kanehisa *et al.*, 2004) pathway name and link to pathway map), protein-protein interaction, structure (with PDB 3D structure image, matched residue range, and % sequence identity for all structures matched at >=30% identity), structural classes (with SCOP hierarchy for structures at >=90% identity), sequence features and post-translational modifications (with residues or residue ranges);
- Family classification: PIRSF family, InterPro family (Mulder *et al.*, 2003), Pfam domain (with residue range), Prosite motif (with residue range), COG, and other classifications; and
- Sequence display: graphical display of domains and motifs on the amino acid sequence.

Family summary reports (Figure 3) are available for PIRSF families, containing information derived from iProClass protein entries (such as membership statistics, family and function/structure relationships, and database cross-references), as well as curated family information, as summarized below:

- General information: PIRSF number and general statistics (family size, taxonomy range, length range, keywords) for all families, as well as additional annotation for curated families, such as family name, bibliography, family description, representative and seed members, and domain architecture;
- Membership: lists of all members separated by major kingdoms and members of model organisms;
- Function, structure, and family relationship: enzyme (EC) and structure (SCOP) hierarchies, family relationships at the whole protein, domain, and

motif levels with direct mapping and links to other family, function, and structure classification schemes; and
- Graphical display: domain architecture of seed members or all members.

To assist with phylogenetic analysis of PIRSF families, the iProClass family reports also connect to taxonomy and tree graphical interfaces. The "Taxonomy Range" field links to a taxonomy browser for interactive display of taxonomy distribution of all family members and phylogenetic pattern of members in complete genomes (Figure 4A). The "Alignment and Tree" field links to multiple sequence alignment and guide tree (Figure 4B) dynamically generated by the ClustalW program (Thompson *et al.*, 1994) based on the PIRSF seed members. The guide tree further connects to an interactive viewer for displaying phylogenetic tree (ClustalW neighbor joining with bootstrapping), protein annotation table, and multiple sequence alignment (Figure 4C).

Integrative Associative Analysis

The data integration in iProClass facilitates functional exploration and comparative analysis of proteins. In particular, when coupled with the PIRSF classification, the iProClass system supports associative studies of protein family, domain, function, and structure (Wu *et al.*, 2004b). Such integrative associative analysis using information on protein sequence, structure, function, and other system biology information is being employed for the protein family curation and annotation at the PIR. This includes drawing on various types of available information to provide a comprehensive picture that can lead to novel prediction and functional inference for previously uncharacterized proteins and protein groups.

For example, Pfam-based searches can identify all PIRSFs sharing one or more Pfam domains. Likewise, SCOP structural classification-based searches can identify PIRSFs in the same SCOP superfamily class. Functional convergence (unrelated proteins with the same activity via non-orthologous gene displacement) and functional divergence (paralogous proteins with differing activities or expression) can be revealed by the many-to-one and one-to-many relationships between the enzyme classification (EC number) and PIRSF classification. With the underlying taxonomic information, one can derive phylogenetic patterns of

Figure 4. iProClass graphical browsers for PIRSF family analysis. (A) Taxonomy browser for interactive display of taxonomy distribution and phylogenetic pattern; (B) Graphical view of multiple sequence alignment and guide tree of seed member; (C) Interactive viewer for phylogenetic tree, annotation table, and multiple sequence alignment

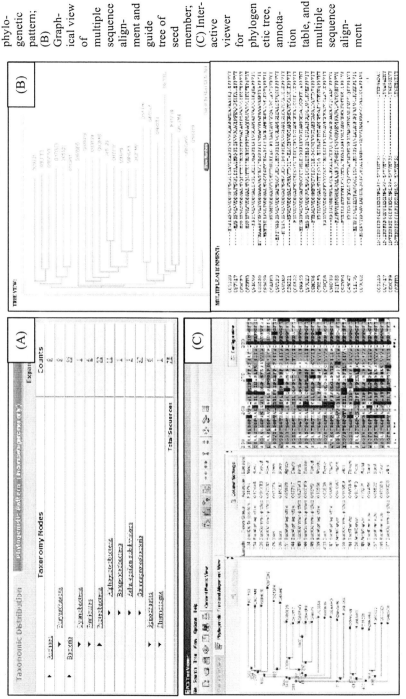

PIRSFs, indicating the presence or absence of corresponding proteins in completely sequenced genomes to identify PIRSFs that occur only in given lineages or share common phylogenetic patterns. Combining phylogenetic pattern and biochemical pathway information for protein families allows us to identify cases where alternative pathways exist for the same end product in different taxonomic groups.

5. Case Studies

The case studies below illustrate how PIRSF classification and iProClass integrative associative analysis can be used collectively to facilitate functional annotation of proteins. The first case shows the annotation of several "conserved hypothetical" protein groups as the subunits of the [NiFe]-hydrogenase-3-type complex Eha, based on genome context and phylogenetic profile. The second case shows the annotation of many CheY-related response regulators based on domain architecture.

5.1. Annotation of Unknown Proteins Using Genome Context and Phylogenetic Profile

The energy-converting hydrogenase A (*eha*) operon encodes a putative multisubunit membrane-bound [NiFe]-hydrogenase Eha in *Methanobacterium thermoautotrophicum* (Tersteegen and Hedderich, 1999). Sequence analysis of the *eha* operon indicates that it encodes at least 20 proteins, including three broadly conserved proteins, [NiFe]-hydrogenase large subunit (PIRSF000230, subfamily PIRSF500033), [NiFe]-hydrogenase small subunit (PIRSF002913, subfamily PIRSF500034), and [NiFe]-hydrogenase membrane subunit J (PIRSF000215, subfamily PIRSF500037). A fourth protein, an integral membrane protein (PIRSF036536), shares sequence similarity to the N-terminal half of the [NiFe]-hydrogenase large membrane subunit (PIRSF006542). These four proteins show high sequence similarity to subunits of the Ech hydrogenase from *Methanosarcina barkeri*, hydrogenases 3 and 4 (Hyc and Hyf) from *Escherichia coli*, and CO-induced hydrogenase (Coo) from *Rhodospirillum rubrum*, all of which form a distinct group of multisubunit membrane-bound [NiFe]-hydrogenases and together are called hydrogenase-3-type hydrogenases. In addition to these four subunits, the *eha* operon encodes three polyferredoxins, ten other predicted integral membrane proteins, and four hydrophilic proteins. All of these proteins are expressed and therefore thought to be functional subunits of the Eha hydrogenase complex (Tersteegen and Hedderich, 1999). Still none of the latter 14 integral membrane and hydrophilic proteins are conserved in experimentally studied membrane-bound [NiFe]-hydrogenases and 12 of them have no experimentally studied homologs in any experimentally studied system.

While only four proteins of the *eha* operon in *M. thermoautotrophicum* can be predicted as membrane-bound [NiFe]-hydrogenase subunits on the basis of sequence similarity to a broad range of organisms, the majority of *eha* operon-encoded proteins and their genome context are conserved in two other complete genomes, *Methanocaldococcus jannaschii* and *Methanopyrus kandleri*. The genome context and phylogentic profile collectively allow us to classify and annotate these groups of "conserved hypothetical" proteins in the absence of other sequence similarity or domain information (Table 2). Specifically, the ten integral membrane proteins and one of the hydrophilic proteins of the *eha* operon are predicted to be subunits of the multisubunit membrane-bound [NiFe]-hydrogenase Eha; and their homologs in *M. jannaschii* and *M. kandleri* are classified into corresponding PIRSF families. The phylogenetic profile of the 11 new PIRSF families and PIRSF036536 (related to the broadly conserved PIRSF006542) shows their strict conservation in the three genomes in Euryarchaeota, with the exception of PIRSF036537 and PIRSF036538, which do not contain the *M. jannaschii* and *M. kandleri* homologs (Figure 5).

5.2. Functional Annotation of Response Regulators Based on Domain Architecture

Prediction of general biochemical functions of uncharacterized proteins is often based on their conserved domain organization, gene neighborhood, and phylogenetic patterns. Protein domain organization is particularly informative for analyzing prokaryotic multi-domain proteins involved in signal transduction, due to their modular structure with various combinations of signaling domains (Galperin et al., 2001). This can be illustrated by the annotation of the various types of response regulators (Table 3), which share the CheY-like phosphoacceptor domain (PF00072) and are involved in signal transduction by two-component signaling systems. In a two-component system, in response to an

Table 2. Genome context of [NiFe]-hydrogenase-3-type complex Eha

PIRSF ID and Name	Mt[*] Gene	Mk[*] Gene	Mj[*] Gene
PIRSF005019: [NiFe]-hydrogenase-3-type complex Eha, membrane protein EhaA	MTH384	MK0477	MJ0528
PIRSF019706: [NiFe]-hydrogenase-3-type complex Eha, membrane protein EhaB	MTH385	MK0476	MJ0527
PIRSF036534: [NiFe]-hydrogenase-3-type complex Eha, membrane protein EhaC	MTH386	MK0475	MJ0526.1
PIRSF006581: [NiFe]-hydrogenase-3-type complex Eha, membrane protein EhaD	MTH387	MK0474	MJ0526
PIRSF036535: [NiFe]-hydrogenase-3-type complex Eha, membrane protein EhaE	MTH388	MK0473	MJ0525
PIRSF019373: [NiFe]-hydrogenase-3-type complex Eha, membrane protein EhaF	MTH389	MK0472	MJ0524
PIRSF019136: [NiFe]-hydrogenase-3-type complex Eha, membrane protein EhaG	MTH390	MK0471	MJ0523
PIRSF036536: [NiFe]-hydrogenase-3-type complex Eha, membrane protein EhaH	MTH391	MK0470	MJ0522
PIRSF036537: [NiFe]-hydrogenase-3-type complex Eha, membrane protein EhaI	MTH392		
PIRSF000215: NADH:quinone oxidoreductase (complex I), subunit 1/[NiFe]-hydrogenase-3-type complex, membrane subunit C/D/J PIRSF500037: [NiFe]-hydrogenase-3-type complex, membrane subunit C/D/J	MTH393	MK0468	MJ0520
PIRSF036538: [NiFe]-hydrogenase-3-type complex Eha, membrane protein EhaK	MTH394		
PIRSF004953: [NiFe]-hydrogenase-3-type complex Eha, membrane protein EhaL	MTH395	MK0466	MJ0518
PIRSF005292: [NiFe]-hydrogenase-3-type complex Eha, hydrophilic subunit EhaM	MTH396	MK0465	MJ0517
PIRSF002913: NADH:quinone oxidoreductase (complex I), subunit NuoB/[NiFe]-hydrogenase-3-type complex, small subunit PIRSF500034: [NiFe]-hydrogenase-3-type complex, small subunit	MTH397	MK0464	MJ0516
PIRSF000230: NADH:quinone oxidoreductase (complex I), 49 K subunit /[NiFe]-hydrogenase-3-type complex, large subunit PIRSF500033: [NiFe]-hydrogenase-3-type complex, large subunit	MTH398	MK0463	MJ0515

* Mt (Methanothermobacter thermautotrophicus str. Delta H); Mj (Methanocaldococcus jannaschii DSM 2661); Mk (Methanopyrus kandleri AV19)

Taxonomy Nodes	SF085010	SF019706	SF036534	SF006501	SF036535	SF019073	SF016136	SF036536	SF036537	SF036538	SF004953	SF005292
▼ Archaea	+ 3	+ 3	+ 3	+ 3	+ 3	+ 3	+ 3	+ 3	+ 1	+ 1	+ 3	+ 3
▶ Crenarchaeota	-	-	-	-	-	-	-	-	-	-	-	-
▼ Euryarchaeota	+ 3	+ 3	+ 3	+ 3	+ 3	+ 3	+ 3	+ 3	+ 1	+ 1	+ 3	+ 3
▶ Archaeoglobi	-	-	-	-	-	-	-	-	-	-	-	-
▶ Halobacteria	-	-	-	-	-	-	-	-	-	-	-	-
▶ Methanobacteria	+ 1	+ 1	+ 1	+ 1	+ 1	+ 1	+ 1	+ 1	+ 1	+ 1	+ 1	+ 1
▶ Methanococci	+ 1	+ 1	+ 1	+ 1	+ 1	+ 1	+ 1	-	-	-	+ 1	+ 1
▶ Methanomicrobia	-	-	-	-	-	-	-	-	-	-	-	-
▶ Methanopyri	+ 1	+ 1	+ 1	+ 1	+ 1	+ 1	+ 1	+ 1	-	-	+ 1	+ 1
▶ Thermococci	-	-	-	-	-	-	-	-	-	-	-	-
▶ Thermoplasmata	-	-	-	-	-	-	-	-	-	-	-	-
▶ Nanoarchaeota	-	-	-	-	-	-	-	-	-	-	-	-
▶ Bacteria	-	-	-	-	-	-	-	-	-	-	-	-
▶ Eukaryota	-	-	-	-	-	-	-	-	-	-	-	-
▶ other sequences	-	-	-	-	-	-	-	-	-	-	-	-
▶ Viroids	-	-	-	-	-	-	-	-	-	-	-	-
▶ Viruses	-	-	-	-	-	-	-	-	-	-	-	-
Total Mapped	3	3	3	3	3	3	3	3	1	1	3	3

Figure 5. Phylogenetic patterns of PIRSF families consisting of [NiFe]-hydrogenase-3-type complex Eha subunits conserved in three complete genomes

environmental stimulus, a phosphoryl group is transferred from the His residue of a sensor histidine kinase to an Asp residue in the CheY-like receiver domain of the cognate response regulator (Stock *et al.*, 2000). Phosphorylation of the receiver domain induces conformational changes that activate an associated output domain. Stand-alone receiver domains (PIRSF002866) regulate their target systems by noncovalent interactions.

Response regulators of the microbial two-component signal transduction systems often consist of an N-terminal CheY-like receiver domain and a C-terminal output (usually a helix-turn-helix (HTH) DNA-binding) domain (e.g., PIRSF002868, PIRSF006171). Phylogenetic analysis of the receiver domains and output (effector) domains of a number of response regulators has shown that receiver modules usually diverged from common ancestral protein domains together with the corresponding effector domains, although recent domain shuffling have also occurred during the evolution of many of these proteins. In addition to the "classical," well-known response regulators consisting of the CheY-like domain and an HTH DNA-binding domain, bacterial genomes encode a variety of response regulators with other types of DNA- or RNA-binding

Table 3. CheY-like phosphoacceptor domain-containing response regulators (partial list)

PIRSF ID	PIRSF Name	Pfam ID
PIRSF000876	chemotaxis response regulator methylesterase, CheB type [Validated]	PF00072; PF01339
PIRSF002866	signal transduction receiver (phosphoacceptor) protein, CheY type [Validated]	PF00072
PIRSF002868	response regulator with HTH DNA-binding domain, NarL type [Validated]	PF00072; PF00196
PIRSF002937	sporulation response regulator, Spo0A type transcription factor [Validated]	PF00072
PIRSF003187	response regulator, NtrC type [Validated]	PF00072; PF00158; PF02954
PIRSF005259	tripartite hybrid signal transduction histidine kinase, BarA type [Validated]	PF00072; PF00512; PF00672; PF01627; PF02518
PIRSF005897	response regulator of heterocyst pattern formation PatA [Validated]	PF00072
PIRSF006171	response regulator of citrate/malate metabolism [Validated]	PF00072
PIRSF006198	response regulator with LytTR DNA-binding domain, AlgR/VirR/ComE type [Validated]	PF00072; PF04397
PIRSF006638	response regulator diguanylate cyclase, PleD type [Validated]	PF00072; PF00990
PIRSF015566	chemotaxis hybrid-type signal transduction histidine kinase, FrzE type [Validated]	PF00072; PF01584; PF01627; PF02518; PF02895
PIRSF026389	hybrid-type ethylene sensor histidine kinase [Validated]	PF00072; PF00512; PF01590; PF02518
PIRSF036382	response regulator antiterminator [Validated]	PF00072; PF03861
PIRSF036383	response regulator with AraC-type DNA-binding domain [Predicted]	PF00072; PF00165
PIRSF036384	response regulator with an HD-GYP domain [Validated]	PF00072; PF01966
PIRSF036385	response regulator, RegA/PrrA/ActR type [Validated]	PF00072; PF02954
PIRSF036392	response regulator, ARR1 type [Validated]	PF00072; PF00249
PIRSF036400	response regulator with C-terminal receiver domain [Predicted]	PF00072
PIRSF036556	response regulator with EAL domain [Predicted]	PF00072 ; PF00563; PF00990

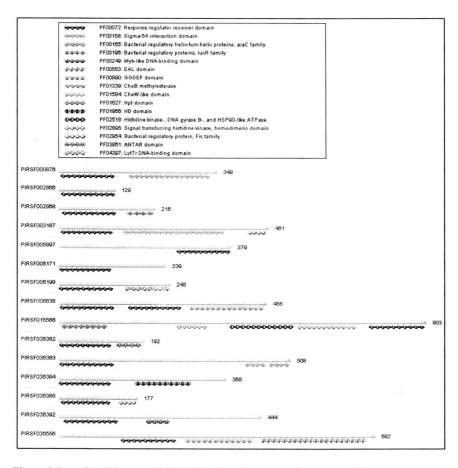

Figure 6. Domain architecture of CheY-like phosphoacceptor domain-containing response regulators

domains (e.g., PIRSF006198, PIRSF036385, PIRSF036383), or with enzymatic domains (e.g., PIRSF000876, PIRSF036384, PIRSF006638, PIRSF036382), or both (e.g., PIRSF003187) (Figure 6).

Because of their complex domain organization, signaling proteins are often poorly annotated in sequence databases such as GenBank—most often just as "sensor protein," "response regulator," or "conserved domain protein." Signal transduction response regulators with unusual domain organization, featuring recently described domains, such as GGDEF (PIRSF006638), EAL (e.g.,

PIRSF036556), and HD-GYP (PIRSF036384), and so-called "hybrid" signaling proteins with very complex domain architectures (e.g., PIRSF005259, PIRSF015566) are among those most likely to be mis- or under-annotated. For example, proteins containing the GGDEF domain, which has been recently shown to be a diguanylate cyclase (Ausmees *et al.*, 2001), are usually being annotated as "GGDEF family protein"—without sufficient information as to the known biological functions. Furthermore, specific biological functions (as opposed to generic biochemical functions) can seldom be inferred solely from the generic functions of the constituent domains, and proteins with different biological functions may have similar domain organization. Therefore, whole protein functional annotation, based on homeomorphic protein families (sharing the same domain architecture and often the same biological function of the whole protein) and subfamilies (sharing the same function), is important for providing high-quality functional annotation.

6. Conclusions

The large volume and complexity of biological data being generated represents both a challenge and an opportunity for bioinformatics research and development. To maximize the utlization of these valuable data for scientific discovery, information needs to be integrated into a cohesive framework. Data integration facilitates exploration, allowing users to answer complex biological questions that may typically involve querying multiple sources. In particular, interesting relationships between database objects, such as relationships among protein sequences, families, structures, and functions, can be discovered.

Such associative analysis of various properties of proteins provides a comprehensive picture that can lead to novel prediction and functional inference for previously uncharacterized "hypothetical" proteins and protein groups. The case studies illustrate that a systematic approach to protein family and phylogenetic analysis, supported by an integrated bioinformatics framework, may serve as a basis for further analysis and exploration of protein function. The knowledge is fundamental to system biology studies at various levels of biological organization, ranging from genes to genomes, enzymes to metabolic pathways, and organisms to communities. The PIR, with its family classification and integrated databases and tools, thus serves as a fundamental bioinformatics resource for biologists who contemplate using bioinformatics as an integral approach to their genomic/proteomic research and scientific inquiries.

Acknowledgements

The project is supported by grant U01-HG02712 from National Institutes of Health and grant DBI-0138188 from National Science Foundation.

References

Andreeva A, Howorth D, Brenner SE, Hubbard TJ, Chothia C and Murzin AG. (2004) SCOP database in 2004: refinements integrate structure and sequence family data. *Nucl Acids Res.* 32, D226-229.

Apweiler R, Bairoch A, Wu CH, Barker WC, Boeckmann B, Gasteiger E, Huang H, Martin MJ, Natale DA, O'Donovan C and Yeh L-S. (2004) UniProt: the Universal Protein Knowledgebase. *Nucl Acids Res.* 32, D115-119.

Aravind L and Koonin EV. (2001) Prokaryotic homologs of the eukaryotic DNA-end-binding protein Ku, novel domains in the Ku protein and prediction of a prokaryotic double-strand break repair system. *Genome Res.* 11, 1365-1374.

Ausmees N, Mayer R, Weinhouse H, Volman G, Amikam D, Benziman M and Lindberg M (2001) Genetic data indicate that proteins containing the GGDEF domain possess diguanylate cyclase activity. *FEMS Microbiol Lett.* 204, 163-167.

Bateman A, Coin L, Durbin R, Finn RD, Hollich V, Griffiths-Jones S, Khanna A, Marshall M, Moxon S, Sonnhammer EL, Studholme DJ, Yeats C and Eddy SR. (2004) The Pfam protein families database. *Nucl Acids Res.* 32, D138-141.

Baxter RC, Binoux MA, Clemmons DR, Conover CA, Drop SL, Holly JM, Mohan S, Oh Y and Rosenfeld RG (1998) Recommendations for nomenclature of the insulin-like growth factor binding protein superfamily. *Endocrinol.* 139, 4036.

Bourne PE, Addess KJ, Bluhm WF, Chen L, Deshpande N, Feng Z, Fleri W, Green R, Merino-Ott JC, Townsend-Merino W, Weissig H, Westbrook J and Berman HM (2004) The distribution and query systems of the RCSB Protein Data Bank. *Nucl Acids Res.* 32, D223-225.

Dayhoff MO (1965-1978) *Atlas of Protein Sequence and Structure.* 5 Volumes, 3 Supplements. National Biomedical Research Foundation, Washington, DC.

Eddy SR (1998) Profile hidden Markov models. *Bioinformatics* 14, 755-763.

Galperin MY and Koonin EV (1998) Sources of systematic error in functional annotation of genomes: domain rearrangement, non-orthologous gene displacement and operon disruption. *In Silico Biology*, 1, 55-67.

Galperin MY, Nikolskaya AN and Koonin EV (2001) Novel domains of the prokaryotic two-component signal transduction systems. *FEMS Microbiol Lett.* 203, 11-21.

Harris MA, Clark J, Ireland A, Lomax J, Ashburner M, *et al.*; Gene Ontology Consortium. (2004) The Gene Ontology (GO) database and informatics resource. *Nucl Acids Res.* 32, D258-261.

Huang H, Barker WC, Chen Y and Wu CH (2003) iProClass: an integrated database of protein family, function and structure information. *Nucl Acids Res.* 31, 390-392.

Hulo N, Sigrist CJ, Le Saux V, Langendijk-Genevaux PS, Bordoli L, Gattiker A, De Castro E, Bucher P, Bairoch A (2004) Recent improvements to the PROSITE database. *Nucl Acids Res.* 32, D134-137.

Kanehisa M, Goto S, Kawashima S, Okuno Y, Hattori M (2004) The KEGG resource for deciphering the genome. *Nucl Acids Res.* 32, D277-280.

Koonin EV and Galperin MY (2003) *Sequence – Evolution – Function: Computational Approaches in Comparative Genomics*. Kluwer Academic Publishers: Boston, MA.

Laskowski RA (2001) PDBsum: summaries and analyses of PDB structures. *Nucl Acids Res.* 29, 221-222.

Marcotte EM, Pellegrini M, Thompson MJ, Yeates TO and Eisenberg D (1999) Combined algorithm for genome-wide prediction of protein function. *Nature* 402, 83-86.

Morett E, Korbel JO, Rajan E, Saab-Rincon G, Olvera L, Olvera M, Schmidt S, Snel B, Bork P. (2003) Systematic discovery of analogous enzymes in thiamin biosynthesis. *Nature Biotech.* 21, 790-5.

Mulder NJ, Apweiler R, Attwood TK, Bairoch A, Barrell D, Bateman A, Binns D, Biswas M, Bradley P, Bork P, Bucher P, Copley RR, Courcelle E, Das U, Durbin R, Falquet L, Fleischmann W, Griffiths-Jones S, Haft D, Harte N, Hulo N, Kahn D, Kanapin A, Krestyaninova M, Lopez R, Letunic I, Lonsdale D, Silventoinen V, Orchard SE, Pagni M, Peyruc D, Ponting CP, Selengut JD, Servant F, Sigrist CJ, Vaughan R and Zdobnov EM (2003) The InterPro Database, 2003 brings increased coverage and new features. *Nucl Acids Res.* 31, 315-318.

Osterman A, Overbeek R. (2003) Missing genes in metabolic pathways: a comparative genomics approach. *Curr Opin Chem Biol.* 7, 238-251.

Overbeek R, Fonstein M, D'Souza M, Pusch GD, Maltsev N. (1999) The use of gene clusters to infer functional coupling. *Proc Natl Acad Sci* USA 96, 2896-2901.

Pellegrini M, Marcotte EM, Thompson MJ, Eisenberg D, Yeates TO. (1999) Assigning protein functions by comparative genome analysis: protein phylogenetic profiles. *Proc Natl Acad Sci* USA 96, 4285-4288.

Porter CT, Bartlett GJ and Thornton JM (2004) The Catalytic Site Atlas: a resource of catalytic sites and residues identified in enzymes using structural data. *Nucl Acids Res.* 32, D129-D133.

Stock AM, Robinson VL and Goudreau PN (2000) Two-component signal transduction. *Annu Rev Biochem.* 69, 183-215.

Tersteegen A and Hedderich R (1999) *Methanobacterium thermoautotrophicum* encodes two multisubunit membrane-bound [NiFe] hydrogenases. Transcription of the operons and sequence analysis of the deduced proteins. *Eur J Biochem.* 264, 930-943.

Thompson JD, Higgins DG and Gibson TJ (1994) CLUSTAL W: improving the sensitivity of progressive multiple sequence alignment through sequence weighting, position-specific gap penalties and weight matrix choice. *Nucl Acids Res.* 22, 4673-4680.

Wu CH, Yeh L-S, Huang H, Arminski L, Castro-Alvear J, Chen Y, Hu Z, Kourtesis P, Ledley RS, Suzek BE, Vinayaka CR, Zhang J and Barker WC (2003a) The Protein Information Resource. *Nucl Acids Res.* 31, 345-347.

Wu CH, Huang H, Yeh LS and Barker WC (2003b) Protein family classification and functional annotation. *Comp Biol & Chem.* 27, 37-47.

Wu CH, Nikolskaya A, Huang H, Yeh L-S, Natale D, Vinayaka CR, Hu Z, Mazumder R, Kumar S, Kourtesis P, Ledley RS, Suzek BE, Arminski L, Chen Y, Zhang J, Cardenas JL, Chung S, Castro-Alvear J, Dinkov G and Barker WC (2004a) PIRSF family classification system at the Protein Information Resource. *Nucl Acids Res.* 32, D112-114.

Wu CH, Huang H, Nikolskaya A, Hu Z and Barker WC (2004b) The iProClass integrated database for protein functional analysis. *Comp Biol & Chem.* 28, 87-96.

In: Trends in Bioinformatics Research
Editor: Peter V. Yan, pp. 59-94

ISBN 1-59454-739-4
© 2005 Nova Science Publishers, Inc.

Chapter III

Bioinformatics Tools for Large-Scale Functional Classification of Proteins – The InterPro Database

N. J. Mulder, T. K. Attwood, A. Bairoch, R. Apweiler, A. Bateman, W. C. Barker, D. Binns, P. Bradley, U. Das, W. Fleischmann, N. Harte, N. Hulo, A. Kanapin, M. Krestyaninova, P. S. Langendijk-Genevaux, V. Le Saux, D. Lonsdale, R. Lopez, J.Maslen, J. McDowall, A. Mitchell, D. A. Natale, A. N. Nikolaskaya, S. Orchard, E. Quevillon, C. J. A. Sigrist, D. J. Studholme, C. H. Wu

European Bioinformatics Institute, Hinxton, Cambridge, UK

Abstract

The emerging field of Bioinformatics is bringing with it a plethora of tools for the analysis of vast quantities of data. Biology in the current era focuses on large-scale experiments to get more questions answered in the shortest time.

Technological advances in the laboratory are facilitating this trend, however, scientists are no longer able to manually decode the incoming data. Data analysis methods now require automation, and Bioinformatics is providing the necessary resources for this to happen. Examples of projects that have increased their scale dramatically are the genome sequencing projects. They are churning out raw sequence data at an alarming rate, and the result is a need for automated sequence analysis methods. The analysis of protein sequences is possible through sequence similarity searches and more importantly through the use of "protein signatures". The latter are methods for diagnosing a domain or characteristic region of a protein family in a protein sequence. They are very powerful for automatic functional annotation of proteins. A number of protein signature databases have developed, each using a variation on the handful of signature methods available. These databases are most effective when used together, rather than in isolation. InterPro integrates the major protein signatures databases into one resource, adding to the signatures with annotation, protein 3D structure information and additional useful links. InterPro groups all protein sequences matching related signatures into entries, providing a useful means for large-scale automatic annotation of these proteins. This chapter describes the protein signature databases, their integration into InterPro, and the applications of InterPro in protein classification.

Introduction

Functional annotation of proteins is an important step in understanding biological systems, diseases and pathogenesis. Thousands of new sequences from genome sequencing projects are available, but cannot be manually annotated due to the sheer vastness of data. Bioinformatics tools provide an *in silico* solution to large-scale data analysis. Reliable bioinformatics methods for automatic functional classification of proteins are being developed, and some have already proven to be extremely efficient. The most useful tools use various methods for identifying motifs or domains found in previously characterised protein families. The two main methods for classification of proteins into families are sequence clustering and protein signatures (in this chapter we define a signature as a "description" of a protein domain or family). Methods of clustering related protein sequences by their similarities are well established and quick, but have their drawbacks. An important factor is the low probability of detecting distant relationships between new and existing sequences of the same protein family. Protein signatures, on the other hand, exploit known similarities between related proteins sequences but go further and use mathematics to describe these.

Sequence clustering methods are generally automated, and assume that members of a protein family will cluster together based on sequence similarity.

An example of a database that uses this method is ProDom (Corpet *et al.*, 2000). ProDom hypothesises that autonomously evolving protein domains can be recognized as shuffled in current sequences by sequence comparison methods. All proteins in the UniProt database (Apweiler *et al.*, 2004), with fragments discarded, are searched to identify the smallest sequence. This is used as a query sequence to search the protein database using PSI-BLAST (Altschul *et al.*, 1997). The sequences that hit become a new ProDom domain family and are removed from the protein database. This procedure is repeated until all sequences are grouped into more than 150 000 ProDom families. ProDom is useful in its high coverage of sequence space, but since its production is automated, the biological significance and annotation of the families may be questionable.

Protein signature methods tend to be more biologically relevant due to the fact that they generally originate from a hand-curated multiple sequence alignment of known members of a protein family. When a set of related sequences are aligned, conserved regions can be identified which may be an indication of their conserved function. These conserved areas of a protein family, domain or functional site form the basis for developing a "description" of the family using several different methods, including regular expressions (for patterns of conserved residues), profiles and Hidden Markov Models (HMMs). A number of public protein signature databases use one or more of these methods, and are described in detail later in this chapter.

Regular Expressions

Regular expressions describe a group of amino acids that constitute a usually short, but characteristic motif within a protein sequence. These highly conserved regions are normally important for function. A regular expression describes which amino acid must occur at each position in the motif. This may be a specific amino acid only, one of a selection of amino acids, or any one except a specific amino acid. The more conserved the region, the more specific the amino acid must be at each position.

Profiles

A profile is built from a sequence alignment, and is a table of position-specific amino acid weights and gap costs. Profiles describe the probability of finding an amino acid at a given position in the sequence (Gribskov *et al.*, 1990).

The scores are used to calculate similarity between a profile and a sequence for a given alignment. There are different types of scoring mechanisms and different ways of using this technique, but the underlying concepts are the same.

Hidden Markov Models

Hidden Markov models (Krogh *et al.*, 1994) use multiple sequence alignments to infer what kinds of residues are likely substitutions at each site in a protein sequence. HMMs are statistical models that are based on probabilities rather than on scores. An HMM is represented by a series of states that can match symbols and transitions between these states. At each state a symbol is matched with a certain probability. Each transition has a probability associated with it that describes how likely it is to move between any two states. An HMM contains many parameters that need to be estimated. These are implemented using the HMMER package, written by Sean Eddy (http://hmmer.wustl.edu/), which allows users to create an HMM from a sequence alignment and to search a database of sequences against the HMM.

Protein Signature Databases

The methods described above have been used by a number of groups around the world for their own purposes. Some have developed databases and software around these and have made them available to the public. The major protein signature databases are PROSITE (Hulo *et al.*, 2004), which uses regular expressions and profiles, PRINTS (Attwood *et al.*, 2003), which uses an adaptation of profiles called fingerprints, and Pfam (Bateman *et al.*, 2004), SMART (Letunic *et al.*, 2004), TIGRFAMs (Haft *et al.*, 2003), PIR SuperFamily (Wu *et al.*, 2004a) and SUPERFAMILY (Madera *et al.*, 2004), all of which use HMMs. Some of these are described in detail below.

PROSITE

The current version 18.25 of PROSITE (April 13, 2004) contains 1257 documentation entries describing 1706 biologically meaningful signatures, which are described as patterns or profiles (Hulo *et al.*, 2004; Sigrist *et al.*, 2002). Both are derived from multiple alignments of homologous sequences, giving them the notable advantage of identifying distant relationships between sequences that would have passed unnoticed based solely on pairwise sequence alignment. Each PROSITE motif is linked to documentation providing useful biological information on the protein family, domain or functional site identified by the signatures.

In addition, there is a collection of 117 pre-release profiles with preliminary documentation that are not (yet) integrated in PROSITE, but available with InterPro (Mulder *et al.*, 2003). PROSITE is in close relationship with the Swiss-Prot knowledgebase (Boeckmann *et al.*, 2003), allowing the constant evaluation of the quality of PROSITE motifs. In return, PROSITE helps to annotate Swiss-Prot entries in order to ensure homogeneity and consistency.

PROSITE Patterns

The first motif descriptors used by PROSITE are *regular expressions* or *patterns*. Patterns describe a usually short but characteristic group of amino acids, or motif, which constitutes the signature of a function, a post-translational modification, a domain, or a protein family. These motifs arise because specific region(s) of a protein which are important, for example, for their binding properties or for their enzymatic activity are conserved in both structure and sequence. The syntax of a PROSITE pattern can be illustrated by the following hypothetical pattern <M-G-x(3)-[IV]2-x-{FWY}, which is restricted at the N-terminus of a sequence (<) and translated as Met- Gly-any residue-any residue-any residue-[Ile or Val]-[Ile or Val]-any residue-{any residue but Phe or Trp or Tyr} (for a complete syntax see http://www.expasy.org/tools/scanprosite/scanprosite-doc.html).

A regular expression is qualitative, it either does match or it doesn't. There is no threshold above which a match can be considered as statistically significant. However, the accuracy of patterns can be determined by scanning a non-redundant randomised database: the number of hits will give a raw estimate of the amount of matches produced by chance (Hulo *et al.*, 2004). The statistics on the number of hits obtained while scanning the Swiss-Prot knowledgebase can also be used to evaluate the reliability of PROSITE patterns (Boeckmann *et al.*, 2003; Sigrist *et al.*, 2002). The numbers of false positives and false negatives give respectively an indication on the specificity and the sensitivity of the pattern. Where it is not possible to build a pattern specific enough, there might be two patterns, which have individually a low specificity but whose simultaneous occurrence gives good confidence that the matched protein belongs to the set being considered.

Despite their limitations, patterns are still very popular since they have their own strengths defining their area of optimum application:

- They are intelligible also for users without special skills in bioinformatics and everybody can easily build their own pattern to search protein databases (i.e. http://www.expasy.org/tools/scanprosite/).
- The scan of a protein database with patterns can be performed in reasonable time on any computer.
- They are well designed for the detection of biologically meaningful sites and the residues playing a structural or functional role are easily identifiable. This quality of patterns is further strengthened by the information contained in the /SITE qualifier of the CC lines, which indicates, among other features, active sites, disulfide bonds, and/or metal and other binding sites in a PROSITE pattern.
- They allow accurate functional predictions. As patterns do not tolerate any mismatch, the occurrence of a match with a pattern centred on an active site indicates that the catalytic function is likely to be conserved.

PROSITE Profiles

Recently patterns have tended to be replaced with the more sophisticated *generalized profiles* (or *weight matrices*), which show an enhanced sensitivity when compared to patterns and are able to detect highly divergent families or domains with only few very well conserved sequence positions. Profiles also characterize protein domains over their entire length, not just the most conserved parts of them. This advantage is used to define automatically the limits of particular domains in Swiss-Prot entries in order to improve the consistency of annotation.

The generalized profiles (Bucher and Bairoch, 1994; Bucher *et al.*, 1996) used in PROSITE are quantitative motif descriptors providing a table of position-specific amino acid weights and gap costs. The automatic procedure used for deriving profiles from multiple alignments is capable of assigning appropriate weights to residues that have not yet been observed at a given alignment position, using empiric knowledge about amino acid substitutability contained in a substitution matrix (Dayhoff *et al.,* 1978; Henikoff and Henikoff, 1992), or methods involving hidden Markov modelling (Hofmann, 2000). The numerical weights of a profile are used to calculate a similarity score for any alignment between a profile and a sequence, or parts of a profile and a sequence. An alignment with a similarity score higher than or equal to a given cut-off value constitutes a match. This cut-off value is estimated by calibrating the profile against a randomised protein database of a given size (Pagni and Jongeneel, 2001; Sigrist *et al.*, 2002). The procedure of normalization used by PROSITE profiles makes the normalized scores independent of the database size, allowing comparison of scores from different scans. The PROSITE profile format allows specification of multiple cut-off levels. The default level zero is used for the classification of matches as true and false positives and negatives, respectively. It is typically of 8.5 (i.e. one false positive is expected in a searched database of $10^{8.5}$ residues) (Pagni and Jongeneel, 2001), but can be modified in order to increase the specificity or the sensitivity of the profile. An alignment with a similarity score higher than or equal to a given cut-off value constitutes a match. A mismatch at a highly conserved position can thus be accepted provided that the rest of the sequence displays a sufficiently high level of similarity. Usually, a second low cut-off level with a normalized threshold score of 6.5 is defined for weak matches, which must be interpreted with caution. In cases where a domain is usually found in multiple copies, the second cut-off level is recalibrated in order to be used to increase the detection of divergent copies. Once a match above the trusted cut-off has been detected in a protein, additional matches under the trusted but above the low cut-off level will also be considered. In some instances, the presence of weak matches in the absence of any strong match is also considered, provided that the cumulative sum of the weak matches is higher than the one of the high and low cut-offs.

PRINTS

Introduction

The PRINTS database houses a collection of protein 'fingerprints' that are routinely used to assign family and functional attributes to uncharacterised sequences. In common with many pattern-recognition approaches, fingerprinting exploits multiple sequence alignments to derive its signatures. The process of building alignments usually requires insertions to be made at particular positions to bring equivalent parts of adjacent sequences into register. As a result, conserved regions or 'motifs' (typically ~15-20 residues in length) tend to become apparent, which often correspond to the core structural or functional elements of the protein. Collectively, such motifs may therefore provide a signature or fingerprint for the aligned family. This observation prompted the creation, in

1990, of the PRINTS database of diagnostic fingerprints to facilitate protein sequence classification and characterisation.

The fingerprinting method involves manual creation of a seed alignment, followed by identification and excision of conserved motifs (up to a maximum of 15 motifs, of maximum length 30 residues) – automatic alignment programs are sometimes used, but errors are corrected manually. The motifs are then searched against the source database, a fragmentless Swiss-Prot/TrEMBL subset of UniProt (Apweiler *et al.,* 2004) using an algorithm that translates the sequence information into frequency matrices (no mutation or other similarity data are used to weight the results). Diagnostic performance is enhanced by iterative scanning, allowing the motifs to mature with each database pass, as more sequences are matched and assimilated into the process. When the iterative process converges, the fingerprints are manually annotated with biological information, literature and database cross references, before accession to the database.

Characteristics of Fingerprinting

The diagnostic potency of fingerprints primarily accrues from the use of multiple motifs and the mutual context afforded by motif neighbours – the more motifs a signature contains, the better able it is to identify distant relatives, even when parts of the signature are absent (thus, a sequence matching, say, three of four, or six of nine, motifs may still be diagnosed as a true match, provided the motifs are matched in the correct order, and the distances between them are consistent with those expected of true neighbouring motifs). The method is thus tolerant of mismatches at the level of individual residues within motifs, and of motifs within complete signatures (Attwood, 2002), and is hence more flexible and powerful than single-motif approaches.

Another distinguishing feature of the fingerprinting technique is that it allows creation of signatures at different 'biological' levels – from domains and superfamilies, to families and their sub-families (Figure 1). This degree of resolution is possible because the manual approach allows us to focus not only on regions of shared similarity (such as those that characterise superfamilies), but also on regions of difference (such as those that resolve subfamilies from closely related siblings within a family, or those that distinguish families from their parent superfamilies). This is important because it is the subtle differences between close relatives that largely determine their functional specificity, and it is just such distinguishing traits that are not captured by methods that rely on matching generic familial similarities (*e.g.*, BLAST or domain-based approaches).

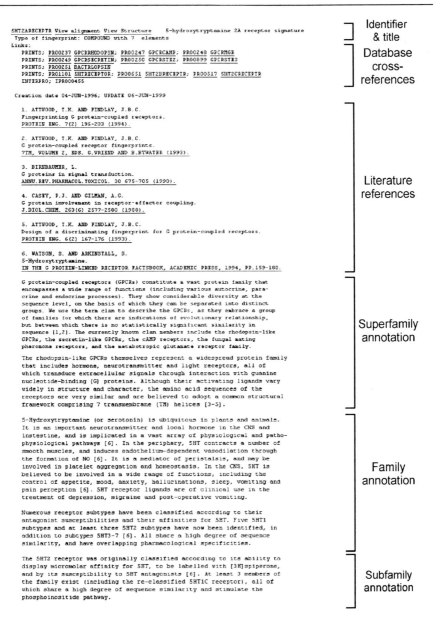

Figure 1. Excerpt from PRINTS entry 5HT2ARECEPTR, a 5-hydroxytryptamine 2A (5-HT$_{2A}$) receptor fingerprint, illustrating its manual annotation, including: an identifier and title; a set of database cross references; literature references from which the annotation is derived; and several paragraphs of hierarchical free text describing the family. The first block relates to the rhodopsin-like GPCR super-family, of which it is a member, the second relates to the 5-HT receptor family and the last paragraph is specific to the 5-HT$_{2A}$ receptor subtype.

This hierarchical approach has been used to analyse a range of proteins, especially those of pharmaceutical interest: for example, to resolve G protein-coupled receptor (GPCR) superfamilies into their constituent families and receptor subtypes (Attwood, 2001), and to finely classify a variety of channel proteins (Moulton *et al.*, 2003), transporters and enzymes (Attwood *et al.*, 2003). Fingerprinting therefore provides a useful complement to HMM- and profile-based methods, which tend to specialise in the diagnosis of superfamilies and/or domain families.

Manual Annotation

An important feature of PRINTS is that, where possible, it provides detailed annotation for each entry. This incorporates general information about the fingerprint (identifier, accession number, creation date and title), cross-references to related PRINTS and other pattern-database entries, and a set of bibliographical references. This information is accompanied by a free-text description of, where known, the function of the family, its structure, disease associations, and familial relationships, the details of which are drawn from, and point back to, the cited literature. This core annotation is augmented, where relevant, with other information relating to spatial and temporal expression of family members, their species distribution, cloning history, and so on.

Where appropriate, the free-text description is presented hierarchically and, if possible, re-used in related entries – the result is a cascade of information from superfamily to constituent family and individual subfamily, the amount of annotation growing and becoming more specific with each step down the hierarchy, as further information is added. Thus, family-level fingerprints inherit annotation from their parent superfamily, to which family-specific information is added, all the annotation of which is then inherited by subfamily level fingerprints. Each fingerprint is also accompanied by a paragraph that includes technical aspects of its derivation (the number of constituent motifs, the version of the sequence database searched, the number of family members, and so on), and descriptive annotations that attempt to rationalise the location of each motif in structural and functional terms.

As the addition of such detailed annotation is very time consuming, PRINTS remains small by comparison with other, largely automatically-derived, signature databases. Overall, however, the precision of the results, coupled with the extent of its annotations, has justified the sacrifice of speed, and sets the database apart from the growing number of non-annotated resources. In this respect, PRINTS adopts a similar philosophy to PROSITE (Falquet *et al.,* 2002) and, in 1992, their curators agreed to collaborate in creating a composite resource – this goal was eventually realised, in 1999, with the first release of InterPro (Mulder *et al.,* 2003), which, by that time, also included Pfam (Bateman *et al.*, 2002) and ProDom (Servant *et al.,* 2002). The bulk of the annotation currently featured in InterPro derives from that of PRINTS and PROSITE.

An Automatic Supplement, prePRINTS

To address its limited size, an automatic supplement to the PRINTS database, termed prePRINTS, has been developed (Attwood *et al.*, 2003). ProDom clusters are used as seed alignments, and motif detection and iterative scanning are performed automatically. The results are annotated using PRECIS (Mitchell *et al.,* 2003), an automated annotation tool that simulates PRINTS manual annotation by creating reports from sets of Swiss-Prot entries, detailing known biological and disease-related information, literature and database cross-references, and relevant keywords. The annotated fingerprints are then deposited into prePRINTS, which serves both as a sequence analysis resource in its own right and as a PRINTS 'incubator', whereby entries may be manually refined before migration to PRINTS itself.

Availability

PRINTS and prePRINTS are created and maintained at the University of Manchester, and are available for sequence and text searches at http://umber.sbs.man.ac.uk/dbbrowser/PRINTS/   and http://umber.sbs.man.ac.uk/dbbrowser/prePRINTS/. PRINTS 38.0 contains ~11,500 motifs in 1900 fingerprints, and prePRINTS 2.0 contains 1510 motifs in 380 entries. PRECIS is accessible from http://umber.sbs.man.ac.uk/cgi-bin/dbbrowser/precis/precis.cgi. The PRINTS fingerprint database provides a potent means of classifying uncharacterised protein sequences at the domain-, super- and subfamily levels, as well as providing a rich source of manually-crafted annotation. These features set it apart from the growing number of signature databases that tend to focus on the diagnosis of domains and superfamilies, and offer little or no annotation. PRINTS and preprints complement both each other and the partner resources of InterPro, each of which has its own unique characteristics and hence offers complementary diagnostic opportunities.

Pfam

Pfam is a large collection of protein families available via the web and in the form of flat files. Pfam is an important resource in the annotation of complete genomes, and is used by thousands of researchers worldwide. The Pfam database comprises two sections: the high quality manually curated Pfam-A, and the automatically generated supplement, Pfam-B. Pfam-A is a large collection of multiple sequence alignments and hidden Markov models (HMM) covering many common protein domains and families (Bateman *et al.*, 2004).

Central to each Pfam-A family is a seed alignment of the protein sequence region covered by the family; that is that part of the sequence within the domain boundaries. This seed alignment contains only sequences that the curator judged to be *bona fide* members of the family. For each Pfam family, two profile HMMs are generated from the seed alignment using HMMER2 (http://hmmer.wustl.edu). These are the ls and fs HMMs, which are optimised for modelling full-length domains and domain fragments respectively. Additional family members are then identified by searching the UniProt-Swiss-Prot/TrEMBL database (Apweiler *et al.*, 2004) against the pair of HMMs, again using HMMER. Each Pfam entry thus contains a 'full' alignment generated by the HMMER search.

Annotation is also included for each Pfam entry in the form of text descriptions and literature references. Also, where appropriate, there are links to relevant entries in other databases such as PROSITE (Hulo *et al.*, 2004), MEROPS (Rawlings *et al.*, 2004), SMART (Letunic *et al.*, 2004) and Transporter Classification (http://www.tcdb.org/). For many entries, the InterPro annotation is more comprehensive than the Pfam annotation and so this is imported into the Pfam web pages and can also be accessed by following links to InterPro from the Pfam site. Graphical representations are provided for the domain architectures of every protein with a match to a Pfam entry. These graphics can now be saved to disk for use in presentations and publications. A number of additional features and links are also included for families including protein-protein interaction data, active site information, and taxonomic distribution.

Just over one-third of Pfam entries contain at least one protein of known 3D structure. In these cases, Pfam provides images of the structures. To make these images more informative with respect to Pfam they are coloured according to Pfam domain and accompanied by a brief description of the structure, followed by the domain mark-up key, which contains links to the family pages for all the domains in the structure. This domain mark-up of structures was greatly aided by the mapping of PDB sequences to Swiss-Prot sequences, kindly provided by the European Bioinformatics Institute (EBI) Macromolecular Structure Database (E-

MSD) (Golovin *et al.*, 2004). Another recent feature, is inclusion of summaries of Pfam domain-domain interactions, which have been determined by mapping Pfam domains onto the PDB structures, followed by the identification of interdomain bonds. See for example:

http://www.sanger.ac.uk/cgi-bin/Pfam/interaction_domains.pl?acc=PF00400.

Pfam aims to be comprehensive in its coverage of proteins predicted from complete genome sequences. Coverage can be measured according to number of protein sequences that match a Pfam-A entry ('sequence coverage') or by number of protein sequence residues that fall within a Pfam-A match ('residue coverage'). Currently (release 12.0, January 2004), Pfam-A has at least 50% sequence coverage for 142 out of 145 completely sequenced genomes and at least 70% sequence coverage for 80 completely sequenced genomes, whilst there is at least 50% residue coverage for only 105 genomes. To address the shortfall, those sequences not covered by Pfam-A are clustered into Pfam-B families. The Pfam-B families are derived from ProDom (Corpet *et al.*, 2000), a comprehensive set of protein domain families automatically generated from the Swiss-Prot and TrEMBL sequence databases, but with those sequences covered by Pfam-A removed. Pfam-B families cover about 24% of the sequences in Swiss-Prot and TrEMBL. Many multi-domain protein sequences contain (non-overlapping) matches to both Pfam-A and Pfam-B families.

Only about 3% of sequences match neither Pfam-A nor Pfam-B. However, the Pfam curators continue to strive towards increasing Pfam-A coverage by discovering new protein families and by refining and extending models for existing families. The process of building and annotating new Pfam families often leads to interesting observations and biological insights. For example, the identification of several novel domains in *Streptomyces coelicolor* enhanced our understanding both of *S. coelicolor* and also general bacterial molecular mechanisms, including cell wall biosynthesis regulation and streptomycete telomere maintenance (Yeats *et al.*, 2003). The automatically generated Pfam-B families do not contain any annotation, but the Pfam web pages do provide alignments, species distributions, and graphical views of domain organisations for Pfam-B families. This information can be valuable to a biologist faced with the task of guessing the function of a protein not covered by Pfam-A. Additionally, Pfam-B families are immensely useful to the Pfam curators as a substrate for building new Pfam-A families and for quality control and improvement of related Pfam-A families.

By extrapolating the current rate of growth in Pfam's coverage of proteins in Swiss-Prot and TrEMBL, we estimate that to achieve 100% coverage, about 25,000 Pfam-A families will be needed, and this goal will be achieved sometime between the year 2012 and 2035.

PIRSF (PIR SuperFamily) Protein Classification System

The PIRSF (SuperFamily) system - based on the evolutionary relationships between full-length proteins - is being developed to assist in large-scale genome annotation, facilitating the propagation and standardization of rich protein annotation. Basing classification on full-length proteins allows annotation of biological functions, biochemical activities, and sequence features that are family specific, as well as educated predictions for both generic biochemical and specific biological functions. The multiple levels of sequence diversity, from superfamilies to subfamilies, reflect different degrees of functional granularity and, thereby, allow more accurate propagation of annotation and development of standard protein nomenclature and ontology.

PIRSF Concept, Definitions and Properties

The PIRSF system is formally defined as *a network classification system based on evolutionary relationship of full-length proteins* (Wu *et al.*, 2004a). The primary nodes (units) in the PIRSF classification are *homeomorphic families* whose members are both *homologous* (evolved from a common ancestor as inferred by detectable sequence similarity) and *homeomorphic* (sharing full-length sequence similarity and a common domain architecture). Common domain architecture is indicated by the same type, number, and order of core domains, although variation may exist for repeating domains and/or auxiliary domains, which are often mobile and may be easily lost, acquired, or functionally replaced during evolution. The families range from those that are ancient and monophyletic (traceable to a last common ancestor) to those that are lineage-specific expansions. A group of homeomorphic homologs may be represented by more than one homeomorphic family.

Each protein can be assigned to only one homeomorphic family, which may have zero or more parent *superfamilies* and zero or more child *subfamilies*. The parent superfamilies connect related families and orphan proteins based on common domains. They may be homeomorphic superfamilies if more than one homeomorphic family exists with the same domain architecture, or domain superfamilies if the common domain regions do not extend over the entire length of proteins. The child subfamilies are homeomorphic groups that may represent functional specializations. The flexible number of parent-child levels from superfamily to subfamily reflects natural clusters of proteins with varying degrees of sequence conservation, rather than arbitrary similarity thresholds. While a protein will belong to one and only one homeomorphic family, multi-domain proteins may belong to multiple domain superfamilies (hence, the network structure). For convenience, Pfam domains (Bateman *et al.*, 2004) are used to represent domain superfamilies.

PIRSF Classification Method

Preliminary PIRSF clusters are computationally defined using both pairwise-based parameters (percentage of sequence identity and the ratio between length of overlap and lengths of the sequences), and cluster-based parameters (distance to neighbouring superfamily clusters and overall domain arrangement). In the next step, a systematic approach is used to define related PIRSFs in an iterative mode that couples manual curation with computer-assisted clustering and information retrieval. In this procedure, all proteins sharing common domains and/or conserved regions in existing preliminary clusters and "orphan" proteins are retrieved and iteratively reclustered based on full-length sequence similarity using varying parameters. Based on the results, curators define homeomorphic families (and other level PIRSFs) based on sequence similarity, domain architecture, and taxonomic distribution.

PIRSF Annotation

The homeomorphic family level is the primary PIRSF curation level – and most significant in terms of annotation and most invested with biological meaning. Curation at the homeomorphic family level includes mandatory text fields (family name, parent-child relationship, membership (member proteins), and signature domain architecture) and optional text fields (description, bibliography, keyword and Gene Ontology (GO) terms). Each family also has a multiple sequence alignment, a phylogenetic tree, and full-length and domain HMMs, all of which are automatically generated from seed members. Families that are used to develop rules for propagating position-specific features (such as active/binding/catalytic sites) have manually curated multiple sequence alignments.

PIRSF for Functional Prediction, Database Annotation, and Protein Nomenclature: What Sets PIRSF Apart

The most important contribution of PIRSF classification to InterPro (Mulder *et al.*, 2003 and to the user community is providing a reliable basis for protein annotation and functional prediction by utilizing two distinguishing features of PIRSF: using full-length protein classification and providing significant amounts of expert manual annotation.

Basing classification on full-length proteins allows annotation of biological functions, biochemical activities, and sequence features that are family specific. In contrast, the domain architecture of a protein provides insight into general functional and structural properties, as well as into complex evolutionary mechanisms, but often not into specific biological function. Sequence analysis and protein classification based on full-length proteins can lead to educated predictions for both generic biochemical and specific biological functions.

For example, members of PIRSF005547 are predicted to be a feedback inhibition-sensitive version of prephenate dehydrogenase (PDH) due to the presence of the ACT domain. The prediction is based on the ACT domain being essential for phenylalanine-mediated feedback inhibition and ligand binding in *E. coli* P-protein (PIRSF001500) (Pohnert *et al.*, 1999). Stand-alone versions of the PDH lacking the ACT domain (PIRSF006786) are predicted to be feedback inhibition-insensitive. Another example is PIRSF017318, where the members contain a catalytic chorismate mutase domain and a unique N-terminal regulatory domain and are subject to allosteric inhibition by tyrosine and activation by tryptophan. Even though this regulatory domain is not yet defined by any domain database, PIRSF classification captures such cases and provides information about the function of this domain.

PIRSF classification can facilitate accurate, consistent, and rich functional annotation of proteins (Wu *et al.*, 2003) and assist with the development of standard protein nomenclature and ontology. Indeed, a classification-driven rule-based automated annotation approach is central to PIR/UniProt protein annotation, in particular, for transferring functional annotation such as functional sites and protein names from characterized members to poorly studied proteins (Apweiler *et al.*, 2004). The multiple levels of sequence diversity improve annotation, allowing for classification of distantly related orphan proteins (usually at the levels of superfamilies and families) and accurate propagation of annotation (usually at families and subfamilies). While annotation can be conveniently propagated for homeomorphic families of closely related proteins, subfamily is most appropriate for larger and more diverse families, especially for more accurate extraction of conserved functional residues derived from experimentally validated members. Standardized nomenclature can be developed based on protein name rules that define standard protein names, synonyms, acronyms or abbreviations, Enzyme Commission (EC) name and number, and even "misnomers" for commonly misannotated proteins (Wu *et al.*, 2004b). The PIRSF names assigned at different classification levels, from more general to specific names, reflect different degrees of functional granularity and can be used to develop protein ontology.

Thus, PIRSF can be used by the scientific community as a tool for such diverse activities as genome annotation, study of evolutionary mechanisms, comparative genomic studies, choosing of candidate proteins for structural genomics projects, and analysis of proteomic expression data.

Accessing PIRSF and Its Current Status

The PIRSF database is accessible from the PIR website at http://pir.georgetown.edu/pirsf/ for report retrieval and sequence classification. The database currently consists of about 32,000 families, including single-protein "families". Over 4500 families containing two or more members have been manually curated for membership and domain architecture characteristic of the family (preliminary curation status). Among them, several hundred PIRSF families have been further curated with additional annotation, including family description and bibliography (full curation status), and are integrated into the InterPro database (Mulder *et al.,* 2003). Because PIRSF classification is focused on the full-length proteins, PIRSFs that are integrated into InterPro are assigned the "Family" entry type.

To find how any given sequence (new or old) is classified in the PIRSF system (in other words, which PIRSF it is predicted to belong to), the *PIRSF Scan* tool or BLAST search (Altschul *et al.*, 1997) can be used. PIRSF Scan is available through InterProScan as well as at http://pir.georgetown.edu/pirsf/ and searches only against the curated PIRSFs. The algorithm assigns any sequence to no more than one homeomorphic family. It is based on HMMs derived from full-length sequences, HMMs derived from component domains, and the overlap length parameter. Users can also perform a BLAST search of a query sequence to get a list of best-matching families (both preliminary clusters and curated families) and of all protein sequences above a given threshold.

PIRSF family reports present membership information, links to other classification schemes (such as Pfam, SCOP, and InterPro), structure and function cross-references, and graphical display of domain and motif architecture. For manually curated PIRSF families, the report also includes additional family annotation and links to multiple sequence alignments and evolutionary trees dynamically generated based on seed members. More than 20 PIRSF fields are searchable, including other database unique identifiers and annotations such as family name, keywords, and length. For example, one can identify all PIRSFs sharing one or more common Pfam domains, or all PIRSFs in a SCOP fold superfamily.

INTERPRO

Some of the major protein signature databases available have just been described. While each of these is useful in its own right, each also has its downfalls, which are inherent in the methods they use, their coverage or their choice of families or domains. Patterns, for example, are very effective at identifying conserved sites, while profiles and HMMs are better for domains or larger regions of the sequence. The user also has the question of which database to use and if they choose more than one, then how to collate the results. They would therefore be far more effective unified into a single resource. InterPro (Mulder *et al.*, 2003) was created by these databases as they recognised the value in uniting their efforts to provide a single powerful protein signature analysis resource. InterPro is an integration of PROSITE, Prints, Pfam, ProDom, SMART, TIGRFAMs, PIR SuperFamily and SUPERFAMILY.

Integration

Related protein signatures from the member databases are grouped into InterPro entries using the following criteria: They must describe the same protein domain or family, and the proteins sets they match must overlap by at least 75%. They should also overlap in their positions on the protein sequence, and not represent domains in different regions of the protein. If the signatures overlap on the sequence but not in the number of proteins matched, then they are separated into different InterPro entries and relationships are inserted between these entries. An example of this is where one signature, e.g. a glucose transporter signature, represents a subfamily of another, e.g. the sugar transporter family, so it becomes a "child" of the latter entry. This is known as the "parent/child" relationship, and it provides a hierarchy of InterPro entries, which helps to rationalise multiple entry hits to a protein and characterise a protein on the superfamily, family and subfamily levels. In this example, it is possible to discern that the protein is not only a sugar transporter, but more specifically, a glucose transporter. Some signatures go further to describe glucose transporter type 1, 2 or 3 proteins.

A second relationship that exists between entries is the "contains/found in" relationship, which describes the domain composition of a protein. The domains must fall within the boundaries of the family signatures and they must have at least 40% of protein matches in common. The relationship is to show the break down of a full-length protein into its constituent domains and explain multiple InterPro entries that are not related by parent/child relationships, but overlap on a sequence. Knowledge about the domain composition of proteins is important for evolutionary studies, and for elucidating the function of a protein. The two relationships in InterPro aim to make sense of protein signatures that have common protein matches and are thus related, but do not represent identical families or domains.

With the above guidelines in mind, curators create InterPro entries based around one or more protein signatures. Aside from information on potential relationships with other entries, each InterPro entry contains a list of proteins in UniProt that the signatures in it match, as well as annotation on the protein family or domain in question. Each component of an entry is described in more detail below.

Protein Matches

For each protein signature, a list of proteins in UniProt that it matches is precomputed. This list gets updated when new proteins enter UniProt or if the signature itself changes. The matches are computed using the InterProScan software package (Zdobnov and Apweiler 2001) described later. The protein matches are available within the entry the signature belongs to along with matches to other signatures in the same entry. The match lists may be viewed in a number of different formats. In one format a table lists the protein accession numbers and the positions in the amino acid sequence where each signature from that InterPro entry hits. The match list may be displayed in a detailed graphical view, in which the sequence is split into several lines, one for each hit by a unique signature. This view includes hits to all signatures from the same and other InterPro entries, thus for each sequence, the domain or motif organisation can be seen at a glance. The bars are colour coded according to the member database (Figure 2). The proteins can also be viewed graphically in an overview, which computes the consensus domain boundaries from all signatures within each entry, and splits the protein sequence into different lines for each InterPro entry matched. Each entry is represented by a different colour and/or pattern. There is an option to display the

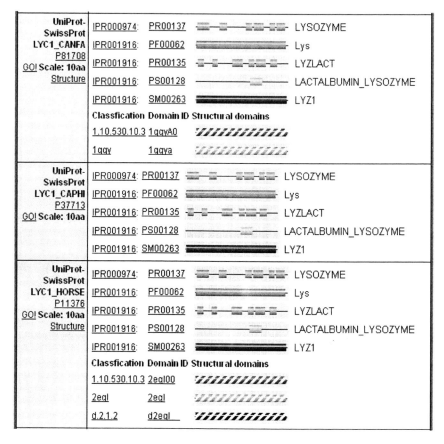

Figure 2. This figure shows an example of the detailed graphical view of protein matches for InterPro entry IPR001916. The view is split into different lines for each signature matched and the structural matches are separated below the InterPro matches and displayed as white striped bars.

overview with the proteins ordered by Swiss-Prot ID, and it is also possible to retrieve this view for those proteins with solved structures in the PDB (Protein Data Bank: Berman *et al.*, 2003) through the E-MSD pages (Golovin *et al.*, 2004). Clicking on the protein accession number takes the user to the detailed view for that protein. For the graphical views a mouse-over displays the actual positions of the matches on the sequence.

Where structures are available for proteins, there is a link from the graphical views to the corresponding PDB structures and a separate line in the display, underneath the InterPro matches, showing the hyperlinked SCOP, CATH and PDB matches on the sequence as white striped bars. This makes it easy for a user to see where the protein signatures correspond with structural chains and to retrieve the corresponding structure or structural class information.

InterProScan

InterProScan (Zdobnov and Apweiler 2001) is a tool that combines different protein signature recognition methods native to the InterPro member databases into one resource with look up of corresponding InterPro entries and Gene Ontology (Harris *et al.*, 2004) annotation.

Applications Included

InterProScan is an application that combines the results of various tools developed to scan the InterPro consortium databases. At the moment, these include:

- BlastProDom (Corpet *et al.*, 1999) scans the families in the ProDom database. ProDom is a comprehensive set of protein domain families automatically generated from the Swiss-Prot and TrEMBL sequence databases using psi-blast. In InterProScan the blastpgb program is used to scan the database. Blastpgp performs gapped blastp searches and can be used to perform iterative searches in psi-blast and phi-blast mode.
- FPrintScan (Scordis *et al.*, 1999) scans against the fingerprints in the PRINTS database. These fingerprints are groups of motifs that together are more potent than single motifs by making use of the biological context inherent in a multiple motif method.
- HMMPIR (Wu *et al.*, 2003) scans the HMMs that are present in the PIRSF Database.
- HMMPfam (Bateman *et al.*, 2002) scans the HMMs that are present in the PFAM Protein families database.
- HMMSmart (Schultz *et al.*, 2000) scans the HMMs that are present in the SMART domain/domain families database.
- HMMTigr (Haft *et al.*, 2001) scans the HMMs that are present in the TIGRFAMs protein families database.
- ProfileScan (Bucher *et al.*, 1996) scans against PROSITE profiles. These profiles are based on weight matrices and are more sensitive for the detection of divergent protein families.

- ScanRegExp
  Scans against the regular expressions in the PROSITE protein families and domains database.
- SUPERFAMILY (Gough *et al.*, 2001) SUPERFAMILY is a library of profile HMMs that represent structural superfamilies for all proteins of known structure.

The Input Sequence

A user can cut and paste or type a nucleotide or protein sequence into the large text window. Acceptable input formats include FASTA, EMBL/SWISS, GenBank or raw text. A raw sequence is simply a block of characters representing a DNA/RNA or protein sequence. Partially formatted sequences are not accepted. Copying and pasting directly from word processors may yield unpredictable results, as hidden/control characters may be present, and adding a return to the end of the sequence may help certain applications to understand the input. The user can input a maximum of 10 protein sequences or only 1 nucleic acid one. Every protein sequence has a checksum (CRC). If a sequence is submitted to InterProScan its CRC is checked against a precomputed list of matches of protein sequences to InterPro entries (that are contained in the IPRMATCHES database). If the CRC of the query sequence matches one in the precomputed results, this result is returned to the user and InterProScan applications are not executed. If the CRC does not match anything, all or user-selected InterProScan applications are launched on the query sequence.

InterProScan Job Submissions

There are currently two ways of submitting jobs to InterProScan: interactively via the web, or by email. A web submission form is available at http://www.ebi.ac.uk/InterProScan/. The email submission address is interproscan@ebi.ac.uk. To learn how to use it the user should send an email to this address with the word 'help' in the message body. A document will be emailed back containing a description of format required.

Email server:

Using InterProScan through the email server is simple. A properly formatted normal mail message should be sent to INTERPROSCAN@EBI.AC.UK the results will be returned to the mailbox. Don't send interactive messages, the software can't handle them! Since InterProScan through email is an automatic process without any human intervention it only understands a limited set of commands. Thus it is necessary to adhere to a well-defined syntax. Some general rules are:

- The mail message must contain only one command per line.
- There is only one mandatory command, SEQ. All the other commands are optional, and default values will be used whenever they are not specified.
- Either uppercase, lowercase characters, or mixed case are acceptable.
- The order of the commands is not important, but SEQ must be the last one, since everything following this line will be treated as a sequence (see below).
- Blank lines or space characters are accepted.

Some valid commands include:

- HELP
- PATH this will normally not be required but if the email server should send the results somewhere else then that email address should be typed here. Example: PATH joe@somewhere.there.
- TITLE a title can be added to identify a search, and should be typed here: Example: TITLE gpr-ii-rpt.
- SEQ the sequence itself.
- END this is required in order to tell the server program where the sequence ends.

Example of a sequence submission by email:

PATH joe@somewhere.there
TITLE My Sequence
SEQ
MMFSGFNADYEASSSRCSSASPAGDSLSYYHSPADSFSSMGSPVNAQDFC
TDLAVSSANFIPTVTAISTSPDLQWLVQPALVSSVAPSQTRAPHPFGVPA
PSAGAYSRAGVVKTMTGGRAQSIGRRGKVEQLSPEEEEKRRIRRERNKMA
AAKCRNRRRELTDTLQAETDQLEDEKSALQTEIANLLKEKEKLEFILAAH
RPACKIPDDLGFPEEMSVASLDLTGGLPEVATPESEEAFTLPLLNDPEPK
PSVEPVKSISSMELKTEPFDDFLFPASSRPSGSETARSVPDMDLSGSFYA
ADWEPLHSGSLGMGPMATELEPLCTPVVTCTPSCTAYTSSFVFTYPEADS
FPSCAAAHRKGSSSNEPSSDSLSSPTLLAL
END

Output:

After a job submission has been validated by the server an email will be sent back to the user with the description of the job the system will run. InterProScan's output currently consists of an email containing a URL, which will contain the results of the search.

InterProScan Output

The output of InterProScan is a RAW document produced by parsing the raw output of each of the applications described earlier, that match InterPro entries. This output is used to generate an XML document that is processed to generate a table and a graphical view of the results. Figures 3 and 4 show the graphical and table views respectively.

A significant difference between the table and graphical view is out-linking to other resources. The graphical view provides direct links to the InterPro entry in both the InterPro database and the SRS indexed version of it, from where the user can link to other classes of databases, which include ENZYME, PATHWAYS, etc. A cartoon that represents the data object for which a match was found, and the relative position of the object follow this in the query sequence. On the other hand, the table view contains information about the family relationships of the matches with links to parent and children entries, if they exist. If a match has been annotated to Gene Ontology terms through mapping of the InterPro entry(s) it hits, the assignments attributed to the object are also displayed.

Downloadable Version of InterProScan

The EBI-based version of InterProScan described above is currently being converted into a full package that users can download for localised installation. A version is available at the moment that already provides the same sets of results and flexibility. However, this version is closely tied into older code that permits full and transparent utilisation of queuing systems (such as Platform LSF, Sun GRIDengine or OpenPBS). This version is available for download from EBI's ftp server at ftp://ftp.ebi.ac.uk/pub/software/unix/iprscan/.

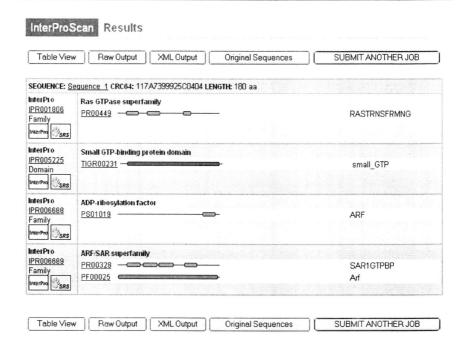

Figure 3. This figure shows the Graphical view of an InterProScan result run on the human insulin receptor precursor.

InterPro Annotation

Each InterPro entry has a unique accession number (which takes the form IPRxxxxxx, where x is a digit), a short name, a name and an entry type. Entries are typed to help the user determine what kind of entry they are looking at, and for internal quality control purposes. The six entry types are: family, domain, repeat, post-translational modification (PTM), active site and binding site. There are rules governing what type an entry should be, and they are manually assigned. A family in InterPro is defined as a group of evolutionarily related proteins that share similar domain (or repeat) architectures, while a domain is an independent structural unit, which can be found alone or in conjunction with other domains or repeats. A repeat is a region that is not expected to fold into a globular domain on its own, a post-translational modification modifies the primary protein structure, a binding site binds chemical or other compounds, which themselves are not substrates for a reaction, and active sites are catalytic pockets of enzymes where a substrate is bound and converted to a product, which is then released. There are

SEQUENCE: Sequence 1 CRC64: 117A7399925C0404 LENGTH: 180 aa				
InterPro IPR001806 Family InterPro SRS	**Ras GTPase superfamily** PRINTS PR00449 *RASTRNSFRMNG*		4.5E-8 [17-38]T 4.5E-8 [53-75]T 4.5E-8 [116-129]T	
Parent	no parent			
Children	IPR003577 IPR003578 IPR003579 IPR002041			
Found in	no entries			
Contains	IPR005289			
GO terms	Molecular Function: small monomeric GTPase activity (GO:0003925) Molecular Function: GTP binding (GO:0005525) Biological Process: small GTPase mediated signal transduction (GO:0007264)			
InterPro IPR005225 Domain InterPro SRS	**Small GTP-binding protein domain** TIGRFAMs TIGR00231		*small_GTP*	70.84 [14-174]T
Parent	no parent			
Children	no children			
Found in	IPR000178 IPR002041 IPR002127 IPR004520 IPR004535 IPR004540 IPR004541 IPR004543 IPR004544 IPR004548 IPR005662 IPR006169 IPR006687 IPR006688 IPR006689 IPR003373 IPR003577 IPR003578 IPR003579 IPR006297 IPR006298 IPR002917			
Contains	IPR005289			
GO terms	Molecular Function: GTP binding (GO:0005525)			

Figure 4. This shows a portion of the table view of an InterProScan run on the human insulin receptor precursor. Note the GO annotation.

also rules governing what entry types may or may not have certain relationships, so it is important that the typing of entries is correct, and this provides a quality control mechanism.

Where relevant, the relationships with other entries are visible in the entry with a link to the "tree" for parent/child relationships, which displays the hierarchy of entries in that tree. This display also includes contains/found in relationships. The most annotation is found in the abstract, which describes the protein family (or domain, repeat, active site, binding site or PTM), its functions, taxonomic range etc., and is derived from merged annotation from the member databases. Where annotation is not provided by the member databases, it is generated by biologists in the InterPro team using the literature and information in the Swiss-Prot entries matched. Literature references cited in the abstract are stored in a reference field in each entry. A list of representative sequences matching the signatures in an entry is provided in the graphical overview format in the "Examples" field.

Gene Ontology

Additional functional annotation is available for many entries in the form of mappings to Gene Ontology (GO) terms (Harris *et al.*, 2004). The GO project is an effort to provide a universal ontology for describing gene products across all species. The project provides a set of terms in a directed acyclic graph under the three ontologies: molecular function, biological process and cellular component. InterPro entries provide comprehensive annotation describing a set of related proteins, some of which may have identical molecular functions, be involved in the same processes, and perform their function in the same cellular locations. Therefore InterPro entries could be mapped to GO terms to provide an automatic means of assigning GO terms to the corresponding proteins. The assignment of GO terms to InterPro entries is done by manual inspection of the abstract of the entries and annotation of proteins in the match lists, and mapping of the appropriate GO terms of any level which apply to the whole protein, not necessarily only the domain described. The associated GO terms should also apply to all proteins with true hits to all signatures in the InterPro entry. Mapping of individual domain or family entries to GO terms provides a means of assigning multiple GO terms to multifunctional proteins. For each associated term the name of the term and GO accession number is given, and these are visible in InterPro entries, with links to the EBI QuickGo browser (http://www.ebi.ac.uk/ego/). In this way, all proteins belonging to InterPro entries mapped to GO terms can be automatically mapped to these GO terms.

Taxonomy

A new feature in InterPro is the "Taxonomy" field, which aims to provide an, 'at a glance', view of the taxonomic range of the sequences associated with each InterPro entry. The lineages were carefully selected to provide a view of the major groups of organisms. The circular display has the taxonomy-tree root as its centre. The model organisms populate the outer most circle. Nodes of the taxonomy-tree are placed on the inner circles and radial lines lead to the description for each node. No significance is attached to the position of the node on a particular inner-circle, other than convenience, though some attempt has been made to group nodes. The nodes themselves are either true taxonomy nodes and have a NCBI taxonomy ID or are artificial nodes created for this display; of which there are three: 'Unclassified', 'Other Eukaryota (Non-Metazoa)' and the 'Plastid Group'. In addition, the number of sequences associated with each lineage is displayed, and in the future this will be extended to include capabilities for downloading these sets of sequences.

Database Cross-References

In addition to cross-referencing the member database signatures and GO terms, there is a separate field in InterPro entries, "Database Links", to provide cross-references to other databases. Included in this field are cross-references to corresponding Blocks accession numbers, PROSITE documentation and the Enzyme Commission (EC) Database where the EC number(s) for proteins matching the entry are common. Where applicable, there may also be links to specialised websites, for example the CArbohydrate-Active EnZymes (CAZy) site (http://afmb.cnrs-mrs.fr/CAZY/), which describes families of related catalytic and carbohydrate-binding modules of enzymes that act on glycosidic bonds, the IUPHAR Receptor Database and the MEROPS Peptidase Database (Rawlings *et al.*, 2004). This provides useful information and links for users interested in a particular protein family.

3D Structural Information

A separate field, called "Structural links", provides information on curated structure links. Though there is no simple relationship between structure and function, it is beyond doubt that establishing structural links (if possible) to sequence based classifications is immensely useful to the scientific community in general. Structural domains (CATH: Orengo *et al.*, 2003 and SCOP: Andreeva *et al.*, 2004) are made up of one or more protein chains in a PDB entry, and the definition may include the full chain or region(s) of chain(s). Currently the links to the curated structural domains in this field of InterPro entries are based on the correspondence between the proteins matching the InterPro entry and those proteins of known structure and belonging to SCOP or CATH superfamilies. Efforts are in place to include only those links where the structural domains overlap considerably with one or more of the InterPro signatures on the protein sequence. In both cases SCOP/CATH superfamily/homologous-superfamily links are provided in the "Structural links" field of the InterPro entry. In addition, at the protein level in the graphical views, all the representative domains at the SCOP/CATH family level are displayed, showing the location of the structural domain(s) in the protein. This enables the user to go straight to the SCOP/CATH classification for that particular domain from the protein's detailed graphical view. Also, mapping between Swiss-Prot/TrEMBL and PDB entries can be many to many, so the "Structure" link displays all the PDB entries associated with that particular protein. Consequently, the user will be able to view the residue by residue mapping between Swiss-Prot/TrEMBL and a PDB chain of interest. This is a very powerful tool, quite unique in its nature, to show such relationships in a compact way.

Applications of Interpro

InterPro is a powerful protein classification and functional annotation tool. The resource has been used in a number of applications including whole genome annotation, automatic annotation of TrEMBL and the Proteome Analysis database. InterPro is used by the genome sequencing centres for annotation of complete genomes and features in the human (International Human Genome Consortium 2001), mouse (Kawaji *et al.*, 2002), rice (Yu *et al.*, 2002), and many microbial genome annotation papers.

Automatic Annotation

TrEMBL is an automated supplement to Swiss-Prot, both of which are included in the UniProt protein knowledgebase. TrEMBL entries are derived automatically from coding sequences of EMBL entries. Therefore, TrEMBL entries do not have the high quality annotation of Swiss-Prot entries, and are waiting to be annotated by curators and integrated into Swiss-Prot. In the mean time, the aim is to provide as much automatically generated annotation in TrEMBL as possible. This is done using InterPro. InterPro entries group Swiss-Prot and TrEMBL proteins belonging to the same protein family or containing a common protein domain. By analysing the curated Swiss-Prot entries it is possible to identify common annotation i.e. those proteins with the same functions. If certain annotation is common to all Swiss-Prot entries matching an InterPro entry, then it can be assumed that the TrEMBL proteins matching that InterPro entry should also contain the same annotation. Therefore, rules can be generated stating something like: If protein hits [IPR00000X], then add [AnnotationY] to the protein entry. The TrEMBL team at the EBI have generated many rules and these are applied to TrEMBL entries regularly to provide, at least, a guess at what the annotation should be.

Proteome Analysis

The other application of InterPro to be discussed in this chapter is in the generation of the Proteome Analysis database (Pruess *et al.*, 2003). The database (http://www.ebi.ac.uk/integr8) provides a comprehensive statistical and comparative analysis of the predicted proteomes (complete protein set) of fully sequenced genomes. It aims to integrate information from a variety of sources including InterPro, the CluSTr database (Kriventseva *et al.*, 2003) and GO Slim. Non-redundant proteome sets are built from the UniProt protein sequence databases, which provide reliable data as the basis for the analysis. All completely sequenced organisms are included, with the only exception of viruses, thus proteome sets are available for archaea, bacteria and eukaryotes. Each organism has an individual page where different statistical analyses, protein classifications, taxonomic information, chromosome tables, comparisons with other organisms and additional links are provided. The whole, non-redundant proteome set is available for downloading in either Swiss-Prot or FASTA format. It is also possible to perform FASTA searches against each proteome. For individual proteins from each of the proteomes, links to structural information databases like the homology-derived structures of proteins (HSSP) database (Dodge *et al.*, 1998) and the Protein Data Bank (PDB) (Berman *et al.*, 2003) exist. Additional statistics, like the protein length distribution and the amino acid composition of a whole proteome, are represented graphically, and structures of proteins can be viewed with molecular visualization software.

The InterPro-based statistical analysis compares the InterPro matches of all proteins in a proteome and derives different lists of the data, sorted by frequency of occurrence or by type of InterPro entry (family, domains, repeats) hit. The percentage of matched proteins in the proteome is shown for each entry displayed. Examples of the statistics available are: general statistics, top 30 hits, top 200 hits and 15 most common domains (Figure 5). There are also precomputed InterPro-based proteome comparisons available in which different organisms, chosen by taxonomic relationship or general interest, are compared. Furthermore, users can perform their own interactive proteome comparisons between any combinations of organisms in the database. An easy-to-navigate search interface allows a user to select one reference organism and one or many other organisms to do a search against. The type of list or analysis required can also be selected.

Discussion and Conclusions

Bioinformatics is a relatively new discipline, but has progressed rapidly as its popularity has gained momentum. Originally bioinformaticians came in from either the biological or computational fields, but now there are specialised training and higher education courses in bioinformatics. This has contributed to the rapid

Proteome Analysis @EBI

15 most common domains for *H. sapiens* [help]		
InterPro	Matches per genome (Proteins matched)	Name
IPR007110	6466(983)	Immunoglobulin-like
IPR007087	2963.3(958)	Zn-finger, C2H2 type
IPR001841	1178(389)	Zn-finger, RING
IPR008938	880(389)	ARM repeat fold
IPR001849	1079(355)	Pleckstrin-like
IPR009057	405(341)	Homeodomain-like
IPR006209	2979(318)	EGF-like domain
IPR000504	1537(295)	RNA-binding region RNP-1 (RNA recognition motif)
IPR008941	690(291)	TPR-like
IPR001452	2202(289)	SH3
IPR008957	942(259)	Fibronectin, type III-like fold
IPR009058	217(210)	Winged helix DNA-binding
IPR001478	1334(208)	PDZ/DHR/GLGF domain
IPR008973	318(200)	C2 calcium/lipid-binding domain, CaLB
IPR000210	491(195)	BTB/POZ domain

Figure 5. An example of InterPro statistics in the Proteome Analysis Database. This table shows the 15 most common InterPro domains for the human proteome.

progress of the discipline. The current era is focussed on genomes and the sequencing and analysis thereof. The sequencing projects are no longer limited by genome size, this is particularly evident in the sequencing of the human genome! However, the downstream analysis of the sequence data is essential for the DNA sequence to be of any use. Proteins, among other materials, are the end products that perform functions in cells. It is the protein function that proteomics initiatives and bench scientists are interested in. It will take a very long time for biologists to elucidate the function of all proteins in the laboratory. This is where bioinformatics excels. A number of protein classification tools have emerged, the most successful of which are protein signatures. Users have been treated by the InterPro database, which does the job of rationalising the major protein signature databases. InterPro not only allows the bench scientist to functionally classify the gene they have isolated, but is used by the genome sequencing consortia for whole genome classification. The data in InterPro is freely available for use and distribution to ensure accessibility to everyone.

References

Altschul SF, Madden TL, Schaffer AA, Zhang J, Zhang Z, Miller W and Lipman DJ (1997) Gapped BLAST and PSI-BLAST: a new generation of protein database search programs. *Nucleic Acids Research*, 25, 3389-3402.

Andreeva A, Howorth D, Brenner SE, Hubbard TJ, Chothia C and Murzin AG (2004) SCOP database in 2004: refinements integrate structure and sequence family. *Nucleic Acids Research,* 32(1), D226-229.

Apweiler R, Bairoch A, Wu CH, Barker WC, Boeckmann B, Ferro S, Gasteiger E, Huang H, Lopez R, Magrane M, Martin MJ, Natale DA, O'Donovan C, Redaschi N and Yeh LS (2004) UniProt: the Universal Protein knowledgebase. *Nucleic Acids Research*, 32(1), D115-119.

Attwood TK (2001) A compendium of specific motifs for diagnosing GPCR subtypes. *Trends in Pharmacological Sciences*, 22, 162-165.

Attwood TK (2002) The PRINTS database: a resource for identification of protein families. *Briefings in Bioinformatics*, 3, 252-263.

Attwood TK, Bradley P, Flower DR, Gaulton A, Maudling N, Mitchell AL, Moulton G, Nordle A, Paine K, Taylor P, Uddin A and Zygouri C (2003) PRINTS and its automatic supplement pre-PRINTS. *Nucleic Acids Research*, 31(1), 400-402.

Bateman A, Birney E, Cerruti L, Durbin R, Etwiller L, Eddy SR, Griffiths-Jones S, Howe KL, Marshall M and Sonnhammer EL (2002) The Pfam protein families database. *Nucleic Acids Research*. 30(1), 276-80.

Bateman A, Coin L, Durbin R, Finn RD, Hollich V, Griffiths-Jones S, Khanna A, Marshall M, Moxon S, Sonnhammer EL, Studholme DJ, Yeats C and Eddy SR (2004) The Pfam protein families database. *Nucleic Acids Research*, 32(1), D138-141.

Berman H, Henrick K and Nakamura H (2003) Announcing the worldwide Protein Data Bank. *Nature Structural Biology*, 10(12), 980.

Boeckmann, B, Bairoch A, Apweiler R, Blatter MC, Estreicher A, Gasteiger E, Martin MJ, Michoud K, O'Donovan C, Phan I, Pilbout S and Schneider M (2003) The SWISS-PROT protein knowledgebase and its supplement TrEMBL in 2003. *Nucleic Acids Research,* 31, 365-370.

Bucher P and Bairoch A (1994) A generalized profile syntax for biomolecular sequence motifs and its function in automatic sequence interpretation. *Proceedings of the International Conference for Intellegent Systems in Molecular Biology*, 2, 53-61.

Bucher P, Karplus K, Moeri N and Hofmann K (1996) A Flexible Motif Search Technique Based on Generalized Profiles. *Computational Chemistry*, 20(1), 3-23.

Corpet F, Gouzy J and Kahn D (1999) Recent Improvements of the Prodom Database of Protein Domain Families. *Nucleic Acids Research*, 27(1), 263-267.

Corpet F, Servant F, Gouzy J and Kahn D (2000) ProDom and ProDom-CG: tools for protein domain analysis and whole genome comparisons. *Nucleic Acids Research,* 28, 267-269.

Dayhoff MO, Schwartz RM and Orcutt BC (1978) Atlas of Protein Sequence and Structure. In: *A model of evolutionary change in proteins.* M.O.Dayhoff, ed. Washington, DC National Biomedical Research Foundation, 345-352.

Dodge C, Schneider R and Sander C (1998) The HSSP database of protein structure-sequence alignments and family profiles. *Nucleic Acids Research,* 26(1), 313-315.

Falquet L, Pagni M, Bucher P, Hulo N, Sigrist CJA, Hofmann K and Bairoch A (2002) The PROSITE database, its status in 2002. *Nucleic Acids Research*, 30, 235-238.

Gribskov M, Luthy R and Eisenberg D (1990) Profile analysis. *Methods in Enzymology,* 183, 146-159.

Golovin A, Oldfield TJ, Tate JG, Velankar S, Barton GJ, Boutselakis H, Dimitropoulos D, Fillon J, Hussain A, Ionides JM, John M, Keller PA, Krissinel E, McNeil P, Naim A, Newman R, Pajon A, Pineda J, Rachedi A, Copeland J, Sitnov A, Sobhany S, Suarez-Uruena A, Swaminathan GJ, Tagari M, Tromm S, Vranken W and Henrick K (2004) E-MSD: an integrated data resource for bioinformatics. *Nucleic Acids Research*, 32(1), 211-216.

Gough J, Karplus K, Hughey R and Chothia C (2001) Assignment of Homology to Genome Sequences using a Library of Hidden Markov Models that represent all Proteins of Known Structure. *Journal of Molecular Biology*, 313(4), 903-919.

Haft DH, Selengut JD and White O (2003) The TIGRFAMs database of protein families. *Nucleic Acids Research*, 31, 371-373.

Harris MA, Clark J, Ireland A, Lomax J, Ashburner M, Foulger R, Eilbeck K, Lewis S, Marshall B, Mungall C, Richter J, Rubin GM, Blake JA, Bult C, Dolan M, Drabkin H, Eppig JT, Hill DP, Ni L, Ringwald M, Balakrishnan R,

Cherry JM, Christie KR, Costanzo MC, Dwight SS, Engel S, Fisk DG, Hirschman JE, Hong EL, Nash RS, Sethuraman A, Theesfeld CL, Botstein D, Dolinski K, Feierbach B, Berardini T, Mundodi S, Rhee SY, Apweiler R, Barrell D, Camon E, Dimmer E, Lee V, Chisholm R, Gaudet P, Kibbe W, Kishore R, Schwarz EM, Sternberg P, Gwinn M, Hannick L, Wortman J, Berriman M, Wood V, de la Cruz N, Tonellato P, Jaiswal P, Seigfried T and White R (2004) The Gene Ontology (GO) database and informatics resource. *Nucleic Acids Research,* 32(1), 258-261.

Henikoff S and Henikoff JG (1992) Amino acid substitution matrices from protein blocks. *Proceedings of the National Academy of Science USA*, 89, 10915-10919.

Hofmann K (2000) Sensitive protein comparisons with profiles and hidden Markov models. *Briefings in Bioinformatics* 1, 167-178.

Hulo N, Sigrist CJ, Le Saux V, Langendijk-Genevaux PS, Bordoli L, Gattiker A, De Castro E, Bucher P and Bairoch A (2004) Recent improvements to the PROSITE database. *Nucleic Acids Research,* 32(1), 134-137.

The International Human Genome Consortium (2001) Initial sequencing and analysis of the human genome. *Nature*, 409(6822), 860-921.

Kawaji H, Schonbach C, Matsuo Y, Kawai J, Okazaki Y, Hayashizaki Y and Matsuda H (2002) Exploration of novel motifs derived from mouse cDNA sequences. *Genome Research*, 12(3), 367-378.

Kriventseva EV, Servant F and Apweiler R (2003) Improvements to CluSTr: the database of SWISS-PROT+TrEMBL protein clusters. *Nucleic Acids Research,* 31(1), 388-389.

Krogh A, Brown M, Mian IS, Sjolander K. and Haussler D (1994) Hidden Markov models in computational biology. Applications to protein modeling. *Journal of Molecular Biology,* 235(5):1501-1531.

Letunic I, Copley RR, Schmidt S, Ciccarelli FD, Doerks T, Schultz J, Ponting CP and Bork P (2004) SMART 4.0: towards genomic data integration. *Nucleic Acids Research*, 32(1), 142-144.

Madera M, Vogel C, Kummerfeld SK, Chothia C and Gough J (2004) The SUPERFAMILY database in 2004: additions and improvements. *Nucleic Acids Research*, 32(1), 235-239.

Mitchell AL, Reich JR and Attwood TK (2003) PRECIS - An automatic tool for generating Protein Reports Engineered from Concise Information in SWISS-PROT. *Bioinformatics*, 19, 1664-1671.

Moulton G, Attwood TK, Parry-Smith DJ and Packer JC (2003) Phylogenomic analysis and evolution of the potassium channel gene family. *Receptors and Channels*, 9, 363-77.

Mulder NJ, Apweiler R, Attwood TK, Bairoch A, Barrell D, Bateman A, Binns D, Biswas M, Bradley P, Bork P, Bucher P, Copley RR, Courcelle E, Das U, Durbin R, Falquet L, Fleischmann W, Griffiths-Jones S, Haft D, Harte N, Hulo N, Kahn D, Kanapin A, Krestyaninova M, Lopez R, Letunic I, Lonsdale D, Silventoinen V, Orchard SE, Pagni M, Peyruc D, Ponting CP, Selengut JD, Servant F, Sigrist CJ, Vaughan R and Zdobnov EM (2003) The InterPro Database, 2003 brings increased coverage and new features. *Nucleic Acids Research,* 31(1), 315-318.

Orengo CA, Pearl FM and Thornton JM (2003) The CATH domain structure database. *Methods in Biochemical Analysis*, 44, 249-271.

Pagni M and Jongeneel CV (2001) Making sense of score statistics for sequence alignments. *Briefings in Bioinformatics*, 2, 51-67.

Pohnert G, Zhang S, Husain A, Wilson DB and Ganem B (1999) Regulation of phenylalanine biosynthesis. Studies on the mechanism of phenylalanine binding and feedback inhibition in the Escherichia coli P-protein. *Biochemistry*, 38, 12212-12217.

Pruess M, Fleischmann W, Kanapin A, Karavidopoulou Y, Kersey P, Kriventseva E, Mittard V, Mulder N, Phan I, Servant F and Apweiler R (2003) The Proteome Analysis database: a tool for the in silico analysis of whole proteomes. *Nucleic Acids Research*, 31(1), 414-417.

Rawlings ND, Tolle DP and Barrett AJ (2004) MEROPS: the peptidase database. *Nucleic Acids Research*, 32(1), 160-164.

Scordis P, Flower DR and Attwood TK (1999) Fingerprintscan: Intelligent Searching of the Prints Motif Database. *Bioinformatics*, 15(10), 799-806.

Schultz J, Copley RR, Doerks T, Ponting CP and Bork P (2000) Smart: A Web-Based Tool for the Study of Genetically Mobile Domains. *Nucleic Acids Research*, 28(1), 231-234.

Servant F, Bru C, Carrère S, Courcelle E, Gouzy J, Peyruc D and Kahn, D. (2002) ProDom: Automated clustering of homologous domains. *Briefings in Bioinformatics*, 3, 246-25.

Sigrist CJA, Cerutti L, Hulo N, Gattiker A, Falquet L, Pagni M, Bairoch A and Bucher P (2002) PROSITE: a documented database using patterns and profiles as motif descriptors. *Briefings in Bioinformatics*, 3, 265-274.

Wu CH, Huang H, Yeh LS and Barker WC (2003) Protein family classification and functional annotation. *Computational Biology and Chemistry*, 27, 37-47.

Wu CH, Nikolskaya A, Huang H, Yeh LS, Natale DA, Vinayaka CR, Hu ZZ, Mazumder R, Kumar S, Kourtesis P, Ledley RS, Suzek BE, Arminski L, Chen Y, Zhang J, Cardenas JL, Chung S, Castro-Alvear J, Dinkov G and

Barker WC (2004a) PIRSF: family classification system at the Protein Information Resource. *Nucleic Acids Research*, 32(1), 112-114.

Wu, CH, Natale, D and Vinayaka, CR (2004b) Functional annotation of proteins. In: *Encyclopedia of Genetics, Genomics, Proteomics and Bioinformatics*. John Wiley & Sons, Ltd. In press.

Yeats C, Bentley S and Bateman A (2003) New knowledge from old: in silico discovery of novel protein domains in Streptomyces coelicolor. *BMC Microbiology*, 3(1), 3.

Yu J, Hu S, Wang J, Wong GK, Li S, Liu B, Deng Y, Dai L, Zhou Y, Zhang X, Cao M, Liu J, Sun J, Tang J, Chen Y, Huang X, Lin W, Ye C, Tong W, Cong L, Geng J, Han Y, Li L, Li W, Hu G, Huang X, Li W, Li J, Liu Z, Li L, Liu J, Qi Q, Liu J, Li L, Li T, Wang X, Lu H, Wu T, Zhu M, Ni P, Han H, Dong W, Ren X, Feng X, Cui P, Li X, Wang H, Xu X, Zhai W, Xu Z, Zhang J, He S, Zhang J, Xu J, Zhang K, Zheng X, Dong J, Zeng W, Tao L, Ye J, Tan J, Ren X, Chen X, He J, Liu D, Tian W, Tian C, Xia H, Bao Q, Li G, Gao H, Cao T, Wang J, Zhao W, Li P, Chen W, Wang X, Zhang Y, Hu J, Wang J, Liu S, Yang J, Zhang G, Xiong Y, Li Z, Mao L, Zhou C, Zhu Z, Chen R, Hao B, Zheng W, Chen S, Guo W, Li G, Liu S, Tao M, Wang J, Zhu L, Yuan L and Yang H (2002) A draft sequence of the rice genome (Oryza sativa L. ssp. indica). *Science*, 296(5565), 79-92.

Zdobnov EM and Apweiler R (2001) InterProScan - an integration platform for the signature-recognition methods in InterPro. *Bioinformatics*, 17(9), 847-848.

In: Trends in Bioinformatics Research
Editor: Peter V. Yan, pp. 95-118

ISBN 1-59454-739-4
© 2005 Nova Science Publishers, Inc.

Chapter IV

Protein Content in Chordate and Embryophyte Genomes

Christian Roth, Matthew J. Betts and David A. Liberles[*]

Computational Biology Unit, Bergen Center for Computational Science,
University of Bergen, 5020 Bergen, Norway

Abstract

The advent of complete genome sequencing has enabled a systematic analysis of the functions required in a genome. Sets of orthologous genes have been determined that describe the basic protein functions found in all multicellular genome sequences to date. Gene duplication and gene loss have obscured the one to one relationship of genes between organisms in some gene families. Furthermore, the rapid sequence evolution of both orthologs and paralogs has enabled the evolution of new functions and the analogous replacement of lost functions. Lateral transfer, including the transfer of organellar genes to the nucleus, has also shaped the protein content of chordates and embryophytes. Taken together, these processes allow a new understanding of protein content and feed into our general understanding of biological systems.

[*] liberles@cbu.uib.no

Introduction

The sequencing of complete chordate and embryophyte genomes has enabled a fuller understanding of the proteins necessary to maintain different types of chordate and higher plant lifestyles. At the time of writing, the human (*Homo sapiens*), mouse (*Mus musculus*), rat (*Rattus norvegicus*), pufferfish (*Fugu rubripes*), and tunicate (*Ciona intestinalis*) chordate genomes are completely sequenced (Lander et al., 2001; Venter et al., 2001; Aparicio et al., 2002; Dehal et al., 2002; Waterston et al., 2002; RGSCP, 2004), allowing assessment of chordate, vertebrate, and mammal-specific functions. Thale cress (*Arabidopsis thaliana*) and rice (*Oryza sativa*) are the only higher plant genomes currently available in a completed state (TAGI, 2000; Goff et al., 2002; Yu et al., 2002). The relationships of these species to each other is shown in Figure 1. Of course, additional information is also available from individual gene sequencing from other species. However, this does not allow for any statements of gene loss or absence of a given functionality from a genome without a complete sequence.

To begin our assessment of genome content, we will begin with some important concepts and discussion of evolutionary processes shaping genome content. Homologs are genes that have diverged from a common ancestral gene. Much can be learned about the processes that control protein function and the proteomes of different organisms by looking at the similarities and differences between homologs, as well as their copy number in a given genome.

It is useful to divide homologs in to two types, based on the nature of the event which caused the divergence. Orthologs are two genes which diverged from a common ancestor after a speciation event, whereas paralogs are two genes which diverged from a common ancestor that was duplicated within a genome (Fitch, 1970). Paralogs can be sub-divided into two types (Sonnhammer and Koonin, 2002). Outparalogs are paralogs that formed by a duplication that occurred before the speciation that separates two lineages under consideration. Inparalogs are paralogs that formed by a duplication event that occurred after the speciation event that separates two lineages under consideration, and can also be referred to as lineage-specific events in this context.

Figure 1. Tree illustrating the relationships of chordates and embryophyta to each other and the major groups within them. Among the completely sequenced genomes, human, mouse, and rat are placental mammals, pufferfish is a teleost, Ciona is a tunicate, Arabidopsis is a dicot, while rice is a monocot.

The distinction between orthologs and paralogs is important because the genes formed by speciation are under different pressures than those formed by duplication, and will have different fates because of this. Speciation does not per se alter the genome content on either derived lineage, while duplication events leading to paralogs clearly does. The distinction between outparalogs and inparalogs is important because it blurs the one-to-one relationship between orthologs. We may have two sets of inparalogs, one in each of the two lineages under consideration, each member of which is orthologous to any other member of the set of inparalogs in the other lineage. Sets of this type are known as co-orthologs. See Figure 2 for an illustration of these definitions.

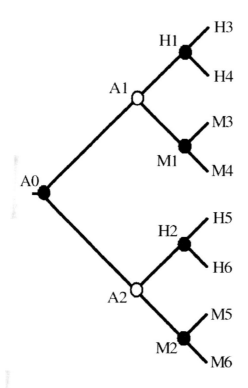

Figure 2. Tree illustrating subclassifications of homology. Letters give species (A = Human-Mouse Ancestor, H = Human, M = Mouse), numbers indicate gene copy. Filled circles represent duplication events, open circles represent speciation events. Leafs represent extant sequences. H3 and M3 are orthologs because their last common ancestor diverged by a speciation event. H3 and H4 are paralogs because their last common ancestor (H1) diverged by a duplication event. With respect to the Human-Mouse speciation event, H3 and H4 are inparalogs, and H3 and H5 are outparalogs. (H3,H4) and (H5,H6) are co-orthologous groups to the mouse groups (M3, M4) and (M5,M6), respectively.

Substitutions in orthologs will tend to be more conservative, since the function of the genes is likely to remain important to both new species. Any changes that arise will mainly be caused by the adaptation needed to colonize a new environment, the relaxation of constraints in a more tolerable environment, or through different fixation of neutral substitutions in the two lineages.

Slightly deleterious substitutions may also be allowed in the short term, if their effect can be reduced by substitutions in other residues that are close in three dimensions. For example, a change from a small residue to a bulky one could be compensated for by a change to a small residue at a neighboring site, so that the stability of the structure is maintained. If this is true, then it would be expected that correlated substitutions would generally be close in three dimensions. Unfortunately, correlations may be difficult to detect because of divergence and diversification (different compensatory mutations in different lineages), high levels of chance correlation, and compensation by multiple sites, and the assumption of closeness in 3D may be broken by long-range compensation and by residues that interact through conformational change. Detection depends on the number of sites that are truly correlated and the degree of correlation at those sites, both of which are completely unknown. Various methods for detection have been developed (Pollock and Taylor, 1997), the best ones incorporating phylogenetic relationships (Pollock et al., 1999; Fukami-Kobayashi et al., 2002), and are often successful in detecting correlations in simulated data. Some biochemically meaningful correlations have also been detected, such as those involving residues brought into contact by the periodicity of the alpha-helix (Pollock et al., 1999).

Paralogs are able to undergo more dramatic substitutions, since the original function of the gene can be fulfilled by one copy while the other one accumulates substitutions. One of four main things can happen to paralogs: conservation of function, neofunctionalization, subfunctionalization and pseudogenization (Force et al., 1999; Zhang, 2003). The same function may be conserved in both copies of the gene, by gene conversion or strong purifying selection, when extra amounts of RNA or protein are beneficial to the organism. Neofunctionalization occurs when the substitutions that accumulate in one copy of the gene chance upon a new function, or a specialization of the original function, such that both genes are now required for the survival of the organism. Subfunctionalization can happen in several different ways:

- the ancestral gene had several functions, and each descendant has become specialized in a different subset of these functions.
- substitutions build up in different parts of both descendants, making those parts unable to make any useful contribution to function. Both copies of the gene (possibly truncated) are now required to perform the function that was previously carried out by one gene.
- the ancestral gene was expressed in several places, and each descendant is localized to a different subset of these tissues.

Ultimately, subfunctionalization can be an intermediate on the way to neofunctionalization. First, subfunctionalization frees up parts of a sequence from constraint that can subsequently evolve a new function. Second, genes encoding more than one function frequently maintain trade-offs between the functions. Dividing these functions between genes then allows each of the functions to become better optimized.

Pseudogenization occurs when one copy of the gene is enough for proper function, and therefore there is no selective pressure to maintain the other copy as expressed and / or functioning. Real instances of recent pseudogenes are difficult to prove, although the presence of stop codons, frame disruption, the lack of suitable control elements, or identification of neutral evolution in otherwise gene-like stretches of DNA have been used to identify relatively young examples (Torrents et al., 2003; Zhang et al., 2003).

Gene duplication itself is a multi-faceted process that involves numerous mechanisms, where a nonexhaustive list would include polymerase error, recombination, and transposition. The resulting duplicate genes from these events are highly variable in both protein coding potential and expression potential (Katju and Lynch, 2003).

Identifying Sets of Orthologs

It is important to note that although we can precisely define the difference between paralogs and orthologs and so on, and the reasons for doing so, it is not so easy to confidently assign these labels to extant genes. These terms are by definition based on the nature of past events, which in most cases we have no direct knowledge of. The features that we are most interested in (evolution of new function, gene loss, analogous replacement of lost function, lateral gene transfer) are perversely what most complicate the picture. Also, in many cases we do not know all the genes of the organism that we are interested in, either because the whole genome has not been sequenced and/or because the genes are difficult to find in that sequence. These problems do not mean that it is impossible to draw any meaningful conclusions, but we must be aware of them when attempting to do so.

Many methods for identifying pairs of orthologs work by looking for reciprocal best matches between genes of the two species in question. If gene B1, of all the genes in species B, matches best to gene A1 in species A, and vice-versa, then these two genes are reciprocal best matches and are assumed to be orthologous. This method is known to result in false positive orthologues (Salzberg et al., 2001; Stanhope et al., 2001).

The Ensembl project uses synteny as an additional indication of orthology (Clamp et al., 2003). Synteny is not a precisely defined term, but deals with homology at the level of genomic DNA rather than that between genes. When several pairs of potential orthologs occur in the same order on the two genomes, it can be inferred that that stretch of genomic DNA was inherited from a common ancestor and therefore that the members of each pair really are orthologous. However, this condition may also hold for paralogs that have arisen by segmental or whole-genome duplication, followed by selective loss.

The Clusters of Orthologous Groups (COGs) project extends the approach from pairs of species to a grouping of genes from the complete genomes of three or more species (Tatusov et al., 1997). Three genes (one from each species) are said to belong to the same COG, and therefore to be orthologous, if each gene is a best match in at least one direction to both of the others. The definition does not require these best matches to be reciprocal, but the three way matching means that real orthologs are still likely to be found. These minimal, triangular COGs are then merged by combining those triangles that share an edge (i.e. a pair of proteins), to give sets of co-orthologs. The COG database was initially constructed from the completely sequenced genomes of several prokaryotes, and was subsequently updated to include seven completely sequenced eukaryotes (Tatusov et al., 2003). This update is known as KOGs (euKaryotic Orthologous Groups). Only one chordate (*Homo sapiens*) and one embryophyte (*Arabidopsis thaliana*) were originally included.

Another approach is to identify pairs of sequences that are likely to be homologous based on some threshold of sequence-similarity, and then to cluster these pairs into families by a simple method such as single or complete linkage. Phylogenetic trees can then be built for these families, and an explanation (speciation or duplication) for the divergence at each internal node can be decided on. This is the approach taken by Hovergen (Duret et al., 1994), and by us in The Adaptive Evolution Database (TAED) (Liberles et al., 2001). Sophisticated phylogeny-based approaches for differentiating between orthologs and paralogs have now been developed (Arvestad et al., 2003).

Comparisons of Proteomes

Analysis of data sets based on complete genomes, such as those in COGs and Ensembl, allow us to see differences on the level of the proteome. (The proteome of a particular species is the full set of proteins encoded by its genome.) Other proteome analyses are also available, such as that at the EBI (Pruess et al., 2003), and the taxanomic data of proteins that match to models provided by the Pfam (Bateman et al., 2002) and SMART (Letunic et al., 2004) databases. Functions that are required or not by a particular species can be identified, and we can also infer the minimal set of genes required for a viable cell, which may also be the same as the set of genes present in the last common ancestor of all the species considered. It is also possible to get some information of this type without knowing the complete genome of all the organisms being considered, by comparing ESTs from the incompletely sequenced organisms to a completely sequenced genome. This has been done for Arabidopsis (Allen, 2002). In this way we can say if something is missing from the complete genome that is present in the others, but not vice-versa. This absence could be caused by gene loss in the complete genome, or by divergence beyond the level at which similarity can be detected, by differing expression levels, or by gene acquisition in the other species.

Gene Families Common to All Organisms

Koonin reviewed the concepts and progress in the search for minimal gene sets of microbial life and for those genes that are likely to have been present in the last universal common ancestor (Koonin, 2003). These concepts are related when comparative genomics, which incorporates orthology, is used to identify the minimal gene set. The minimal set of genes for a functioning organism in a particular environment is that where every member is essential to the survival of the organism. This can be searched for by comparing the complete genomes of distantly related organisms under the assumption that any sets of orthologs that are found are likely to represent essential functions. However, this assumption is complicated by essential processes being carried out by non-orthologous protein families in different organisms, meaning that it is more appropriate to discuss a minimal functional set.

Gene loss can also be used to explain some of the features that are explainable by horizontal gene transfer, but we have no reliable estimate of the relative rates of these two processes. Having said all that, most of the genes that are ubiquitous are associated with translation, some with transcription, and some with replication and repair (Koonin, 2003). The problems described should be less significant when looking at more recent groups such as chordates and embryophytes.

Chordate-Specific Gene Families

Chordates consist of the urochordates (tunicates), the cephalochordates, and the vertebrates. The branch leading to the tunicates is thought to have separated first. Comparison of a tunicate genome, such as that of *Ciona intestinalis* (Dehal et al., 2002), to genomes of chordates from the other two classes should therefore allow insights into the origin of chordates.

There is evidence for large scale gene expansions, possibly by one or more rounds of whole genome duplication, along the branch leading to the vertebrates after it separated from that leading to the tunicates (Ohno, 1970; Leveugle et al., 2004). However, there are also derived characteristics in the tunicate genome, and so it does not directly represent the chordate ancestral genome (Leveugle et al., 2004). Some studies argue that there are often four vertebrate orthologs of each invertebrate gene, that paralogs cluster in similar ways in different regions of the genome, and that these two things indicate that there have been two rounds of gene duplication in the evolution of vertebrates since they diverged from the other chordates. This is known as the 2R hypothesis of vertebrate evolution, and is still controversial. The value of the one-to-four rule has been disputed, even if this ratio is observed, since gene family size alone does not say whether the increase arose by gene or genome duplication (Hokamp et al., 2003). Others have concluded that there are not enough families to which this rule applies anyway, and that those families that do show this ratio do not usually show the only phylogenetic tree topology that is consistent with 2R (Hughes and Friedman, 2003). Given the unexpectedly rapid dynamics of gene duplication and gene loss, it may be difficult to resolve this issue even with additional genome sequences (Lynch and Conery, 2000).

The draft genome of Ciona was annotated by comparison to known proteins and to Ciona ESTs (Dehal et al., 2002). The authors caution that the genome sequence and thus its annotation are in draft format. This has been high-lighted by evidence for globin genes that did not show up in the draft (Clark et al., 2003), for example. However the general conclusions from their annotation are still valid. Relative to Ciona, the human genome was found to have notably more zinc-finger binding domains, more immunoglobulin domains, and more GPCR (G-protein Coupled Receptor) domains, reflecting vertebrate innovations in adaptive immunity, intercellular signaling, and the nervous system. It was also found that there were many more lineage-specific duplications in vertebrates than in tunicates, suggesting that the Ciona genome approximates the genome of the ancestral chordate. However, some tunicate features, such as the arrangement of

Hox genes (Spagnuolo et al., 2003), show evidence of being unconstrained. This is not seen in Amphioxus (a cephalochordate), which suggests that the relaxation is a derived characteristic rather than ancestral, and that Amphioxus might better represent the ancestral chordate genome (Holland and Gibson-Brown, 2003). The combination of ancestral and derived characteristics is likely to occur in all extant genomes however (since they've been evolving for equal amounts of time, albeit under different selective regimes), which really means that the more we have, the better our understanding of chordate evolution will be.

Some patterns emerged when genes involved in major sets of functions, such as signaling, immunity, and the central nervous system, were compared between Ciona and other genomes (Dehal et al., 2002). The endocrine (chemical communication) system has some features that appear to be vertebrate specific (steroid hormones and their receptors) since no orthologs are found in Ciona, some that appear to be chordate specific (eg. thyroid hormone receptors) since no orthologs are found in Drosophila, some that pre-date the origin of chordates (nuclear receptors) since they are found in Drosophila, and some that appear to be tunicate innovations (for example, a previously unidentified family of glycoprotein hormone receptors). In contrast, Ciona does not have the adaptive immune system that is characteristic of vertebrates, unless it has highly divergent orthologs of these that have not been identified. However, it does share some protein domains in common with the vertebrate innate immunity system, although in previously unknown combinations. In contrast, several genes involved in the central nervous system of vertebrates have orthologs in Ciona, suggesting that they are chordate characteristics.

Large increases in the numbers of genes of a particular type often allow major innovations in organisms. Examples of such lineage specific expansions in chordates include vertebrate olfactory receptors, vertebrate HOX genes and GABA-A receptors in mammals.

Olfactory receptors are members of the G-protein coupled receptor (GPCR) family. There are more than 1000 olfactory receptor genes in mammals, most of which are functioning genes in mice but two thirds of which appear to be pseudogenes in humans (Gilad et al., 2003). This reflects the importance of the sense of smell in rodents and presumably the common ancestor of all mammals, and its declining importance in primates.

HOX genes control development in metazoans, and the expansion of the HOX gene family in vertebrates is linked to the increased developmental complexity of vertebrates (Pendleton et al., 1993; Wagner et al., 2003) with respect to Ciona and to non-chordates such as Drosophila.

GABA is the primary inhibitory neurotransmitter in the mammalian central nervous system (Whiting et al., 1999). GABA-A is a ligand-gated ion-channel to which GABA binds, allowing the transport of calcium ions. The expansion of this family parallels the increased complexity of the mammalian brain.

The patterns of gene loss, lineage-specific innovation, whole genome duplication and so on that have shaped chordate evolution, and the relative importance of these processes remain unclear. Additional genomes from increasingly closely related species will enable better understanding.

Embryophyte-Specific Gene Families

There is less information about the gene content of embryophytes than there is about chordates because of less genomic sequencing. The gene content of *Arabidopsis thaliana* was first analyzed by comparison to other dicot species where large EST sets were available (TAGI, 2000; Allen, 2002). The three species chosen for the comparison were the Rosids *Glycine max* (soybean), *Medicago truncatula* (barrel medic) and the Asterid *Lycopersicon esculentum* (tomato). The presence/absence of a gene may be caused by gene loss in Arabidopsis, divergence beyond a level at which similarity can be detected, or gene acquisition by the other species. This comparison showed that between 10 and 15% of the expressed sequences from the three test species had no detectable homolog in Arabidopsis. But 545 of the 2077 undetectable soybean sequences had homologs in Medicago. As an example, two tomato families that had no detectable homolog in Arabidopsis but were found in soybean and Medicago are discussed in more detail, polyphenol oxidase (PPO) and ornithine decarboxylase (ODC).

PPOs are responsible for enzymatic postharvest browning, and widely distributed in the plant kingdom. Tomato contains at least 7, soybean 4 and Medicago one, but there is no homolog found in Arabidopsis. ODCs catalyze the conversion of ornithine to putrescine which is then transformed into polyamines, like spermidine and spermine (Davis et al., 1992). Polyamines play a crucial structural role in stabilizing anionic species, like DNA. This makes them essential to plants in development, particularly in root growth, flower differentiation, and in plant defense, such as in the synthesis of nicotine (Kumar et al., 1996; Watson et al., 1998; Allen, 2002; Walters, 2003).

In plants and bacteria there is a separate pathway for the biosynthesis of polyamines where arginine is converted to agmatine by arginine decarboxylase (ADC), which subsequently is converted to putrescine. Most plants have both activities, but some of the organisms have lost one or the other. Although ADC and ODC serve only partially overlapping functions, one activity or the other seems to be dispensable in some organisms, particularly those under selection for reduced genome size. The lack of ODC in Arabidopsis has also been confirmed biochemically (Watson et al., 1998).

The recent publication of two draft genomes of rice (*Oryza sativa indica* and *japonica* (Goff et al., 2002; Yu et al., 2002)) allows a comparison between the gene content of monocots and dicots. A striking asymmetry was found in this monocot-eudicot analysis. In the indica cultivar, 80.6% of the Arabidopsis genes had a homolog with a mean detectable homology over 80.1% of the protein lengths and 60.0% amino acid identity. In contrast, only 49.4% of all predicted rice genes had a homolog in Arabidopsis with homology detectable over 77.8% of protein lengths and 57.8% amino acid identity (Yu et al., 2002).

In the japonica cultivar less strict rules seem to have been applied (Goff, et al., 2002), but the asymmetry remains. 85% of Arabidopsis genes have a homolog at a mean amino acid identity of 49.5%. For japonica, only 49.1% of the predicted genes were found. The discrepancy can partially be explained by the poor quality of the predicted genes and by an observed difference in GC-content and codon usage in rice, making it difficult to detect ancient homologs. Also, the genome content of rice is preliminary and subject to some modification.

About 8000 Arabidopsis predicted proteins can be found in rice, but not in Drosophila, nematodes, yeast, or any sequenced bacterial genomes. For 13000 of the predicted rice genes the same observation applies; they can be found in Arabidopsis, but not in the other genomes. In addition, 4000 predicted Arabidopsis proteins lack significant homology to any predicted rice genes and are not found in genome sequences of other organisms, which suggests that some of these may be dicot-specific (Goff et al., 2002).

The completion of additional plant genomes together with the already existing animal genomes may help to solve one great mystery of the last common ancestor of plants and animals: was it unicellular or multicellular? Evidence for a unicellular origin can be found by analyzing pattern formation in the two kingdoms (Meyerowitz, 2002). In Drosophila, as animal example, segmental identity is established by the spatially specific transcriptional activation of an overlapping series of HOX homeobox genes. A similar process occurs in the specification of the radial pattern in Arabidopsis flowers, but the master regulatory genes are MADS box transcripton factors. Homeobox and MADS box transcription factor genes are not homologous: There is no detectable similarity in their amino acid sequences, and the protein structures share no resemblance . Although animals contain MADS box genes, they only have a few and none of them is involved in pattern formation. The same is true for the homeobox genes in plants; they exist, but mutations in these genes don't show homeotic phenotypes. It seems that plants and animals developed pattern formation independently starting with transcription factor families present in the last common ancestor.

Lateral Gene Transfer

Lateral or horizontal gene transfer (LGT), the exchange of genes across mating barriers, has become an important and widely discussed subject. Detection of LGT is not an easy task and results very often in false positive identification (see below; Kurland et al., 2003). The safest method of detection is by comparing gene phylogenies to species phylogeny and picking the cases where an unlikely pattern of gene duplication and selective loss would have to be inferred.

In bacteria LGT is a highly significant process; comparison and analysis of the genomes of *Escherichia coli* and *Salmonella enterica* show that most of the phenotypic characteristics distinguishing *E. coli* from *S. enterica* have been horizontally transferred. The acquisition of genetic material by LGT occurred at about 16 kb/Myr since the divergence of the two species ca. 100 Myr ago. At the same time chromosome lengths are conserved in these bacteria which implies that increases in genome size due to the acquisition of horizontally transferred genes are offset by equivalent losses of DNA through deletion (Lawrence and Ochman, 1998). LGT has furthermore been responsible in the development and rapid spreading of multi drug resistances in human pathogenic bacteria. LGT and subsequent loss of DNA create extremely dynamic microbial genomes (Doolittle, 1999; Ochman et al., 2000; Lawrence and Hendrickson, 2003). Although we can see highly dynamic genomes in prokaryotes, the exchange of genetic material by LGT is influenced by several factors. The most significant are genome size, G/C content, carbon utilization and oxygen tolerance. Organisms preferably exchange genes with other organisms in a similar environment. For example, heterotrophic organisms exchange genes to utilize a new carbon source (Jain et al., 2003).

In contrast to prokaryotes, eukaryotes seem to be rather immune to LGT. Only a few examples of prokaryote to eukaryote LGT events have been described. The known examples show transfer from prokaryotic organisms to single cellular eukaryotes: enzymes from the isoprenoid biosynthesis pathways from a bacterium to a diplomonad (Boucher and Doolittle, 2000), N-acetylneuraminate lyase from vertebrate parasitic bacteria to *Trichomonas vaginalis* (de Koning et al., 2000), fermentation enzymes from bacteria and archea to *Entamoeba histolytica* (Field et al., 2000), glucose kinase from bacteria to diplomonads (Henze et al., 2001), phosphoenolpyruvate carboxykinase from archea to *Giardia intestinalis* (Suguri et al., 2001), and sulfide dehydrogenase from bacteria to diplomonads (Andersson and Roger, 2002). All these cases seem to be single species specific transfers. Only one case (glutamate synthase) has an impact on a wider range of eukaryotes and is thought to have happened early in evolution. (Andersson and Roger, 2002).

In higher eukaryotes LGT is less likely to be passed on due to the germ-soma separation. In the few documented cases, there is a clear difference between animals and plants. Analysis of the available vertebrate genomes shows no support for LGT from bacteria to vertebrates (Salzberg et al., 2001; Stanhope et al., 2001).

In plants, several examples of LGT have been documented. The genus Nicotiana contains sequences transferred from *Agrobacterium rhizogenes*. It has been known for many years that infected *Nicotiana glauca* contained sequences homologous to regions of the Ri-plasmid of *A. rhizogenes* (White et al., 1983). Later it was also shown that several other species in the subgeni Rustica, Tabacum, and Petunioides contain at least one of the genes discovered in *N. glauca*. Of the 4 genes analyzed, only 2 were also expressed in leaves of mature plants, whereas most of the genes are expressed in hormone-autotrophic callus tissue. (Intrieri and Buiatti, 2001).

Several cases of lateral transfer of mitochondrial genes or introns have been reported. Cho and coworkers (1998) reported an explosive invasion of plant mitochondria by a group I intron. Group I introns are mobile, self-splicing genetic elements that are principally found in organellar genomes of fungi and lower plants and nuclear rRNA genes. In vascular plants, the distribution of a group I intron in the cox1 gene is highly disjunct and indicates that the intron has been acquired recently and in several events from a fungal source into angiosperms.

A second case of intron transfer has been reported for a Southeast Asian clade of Gnetum. Most of these species contain a second group II intron in the nad1 gene (group II introns are self-splicing genetic elements with a different splicing mechanims from group I introns). This second intron copy shows the highest homology to euasterids and indicates therefore a LGT from angiosperms to gymnosperms (Won and Renner, 2003).

In an additional study, Bergthorsson and coworkers (2003) identified two ribosomal protein genes that were absent from the mitochondrial genomes of most of the members of a vast eudicot clade. The vast amount of gene loss inferred if the genes were retained in the mtDNA of these few species indicates a horizontal reacquisition by LGT. This is also confirmed by the analysis of the gene sequences which showed a phylogeny not in accordance with the species phylogeny. The kiwifruit *rps2* gene clustered with monocot genes, and the honeysuckel *rps11* gene (Caprifoliaceae) nested within the Ranunculales. In *Sanguinaria canadensis* (bloodroot, Papaveraceae, eudicot) the *rps11* gene is chimeric; its 5' half is of expected vertical origin, but the 3' half is clearly of monocot origin. This acquisition seems to be rather recent, as other genera of Papaveraceae contain only a non-chimeric eudicot gene.

A pharmaceutically interesting case of lateral transfer has been reported from yew (Taxus) species. Taxol is a highly functionalized diterpenoid. This compound was the world's first billion dollar anticancer drug. Extracting taxol from the highly endangered yew trees makes these drug expensive and unavailable to many people worldwide (Strobel, 2003). Organic synthesis is not an economically viable alternative (Nicolau et al., 1994). Another possible source was located in endophytes living on virtually all higher plants. In 1993 a taxol-producing endophytic fungus was isolated from *Taxus brevifolia* (Strobel et al., 1993). As the first taxol-producing endophyte had been isolated from a taxol producing plant it was inferred that lateral transfer of the genes for taxol synthesis from the plant to the fungus had occurred. More recent discoveries of a wide variety of taxol producing fungi on a variety of taxol producing plants all around the world, indicate that this compound may have its origins in fungi, and if there is lateral transfer it may have been from the microbe to the higher plant (Strobel, 2003).

Another type of LGT is intercellular gene transfer (IGT), the transfer of genetic material from organelles to the nucleus. IGT happens in all eukaryotic cells. Two independent studies showed that a neomycine resistance gene introduced into tobacco chloroplast was transferred into the nucleus at a significant rate (Huang et al., 2003; Stegeman et al., 2003). The transfer probably involves the disruption of chloroplast and the uptake of the released DNA into the nucleus. Support for this kind of mechanism comes from a similar experiment with the single cellular algae *Chlamydomonas reinhardtii*, which contains only a single chloroplast and does not show any significant transfer of antibiotic resistance to the nucleus. There is also no detectable trace of chloroplastic genes in the *C. reinhardtii* genome (Lister et al., 2003). Plants with numerous chloroplasts show different amounts of chloroplastic DNA in their genomes. Arabidopsis contains only a total of about 11kb of integrated chloroplastic DNA, whereas rice contains a recent insertion of 33kb and an additional 131kb insertion, corresponding to nearly the entire plastid genome. Transfer from mitochondria is even more abundant. Arabidopsis chromosome 2 contains a complete 367kb copy of the mitochondrial genome, and rice chromosome 10 contains 57 fragments of mtDNA ranging from 80 to 2500 bp in length. The yeast genome contains 34 small fragments of mitochondrial DNA, and even the human genome contains 59 fragments of mitochondrial DNA > 2kb, including one 14.6 kb nearly complete copy of the human mitochondrial genome. (Martin, 2003).

Comparisons within Gene Families

When whole genomes are not available for all the species we are considering, such as in TAED (Liberles et al., 2001), we cannot infer much from the presence or absence of a particular species in a particular gene family. However, we can say a lot about the patterns of amino acid substitutions along branches of the phylogenetic trees of each family. (Though in some cases it may be necessary to sequence homologs in additional related species to tie these changes to a particular evolutionary event.) A feature of TAED is the availability of the ratio of non-synonymous to synonymous substitutions (Ka/Ks) for each branch of every phylogenetic tree. In the absence of selective pressure on the protein, the rate of non-synonymous substitution should be the same as the rate of synonymous substitution. If there has been pressure to change the amino acid sequence (positive selection), for example, for a protein playing a role in adaptation to a new environment, then Ka/Ks will be greater than one. Conversely, if there has been pressure to preserve the amino acid sequence (negative selection), then Ka/Ks will be less than one. The average Ka/Ks ratio for human and rodent sequences is around 0.2, indicating that most proteins are under strong negative selection. This is not surprising, given that proteins have been selected through billions of years of evolution to perform specific biochemical functions. Between 1 and 5% of branches averaged over all gene families may show evidence for positive selection or relaxation of selective constraint without pseudogenization (Liberles et al., 2001). There is, of course, a large degree of gene family-specific variance.

Another approach for detecting positive selective pressures is to look for a shift in substitution model. Specific likelihood ratio tests can be utilized to look for significant shifts in parameters along various branches of a phylogenetic tree. The shape parameter, alpha, of the gamma distribution of amino acid rates across sites is the most common parameter to analyze in this context (Gaucher et al., 2002). Other parameters, like the optimum substitution matrix in G-protein coupled receptors (Soyer et al., 2003) or more general nucleotide substitution parameters along specific lineages (Ota and Penny, 2003) have also been used to detect significant shifts.

Case Studies

Some interesting examples of positive selection have emerged, where function may have changed between orthologs in a genome. One case showing a novel mechanism is selection on voltage-gated calcium channels for indel events that regulate protein length (which effects activity) between various primate species (Podlaha and Zhang, 2003). However, there are many interesting cases involving positive selection on substitution.

One such case is leptin, also a primate-specific example. Leptin was identified as the obesity gene in mice, where leptin deficient mice are obese, but are cured with leptin treatment. However, the role of leptin in humans did not appear to be so simple (Benner et al., 1998). Both Ka/Ks and analysis of alpha in the leptin gene family tree offered some indications of primate-specific evolution (Benner et al., 1998; Liberles et al., 2001; Siltberg and Liberles, 2002). Additionally, the extracellular domain of the leptin receptor showed similar patterns of positive selection to leptin (Benner et al., 1998). Evidence for transposon-mediated changes in the expression of leptin and its receptor during the primate lineage (novel expression in placenta) has emerged (Bi et al., 1997; Kapitonov and Jurka, 1999). Using a combination of substitution patterns and structure, a novel primate-specific binding site in leptin has been proposed (Gaucher et al., 2003). Further, the binding interface of leptin with its receptor, as modeled computationally (Hiroike et al., 2000) appears to have undergone radical substitution. Leptin appears to be a case where primate genes have undergone some neofunctionalization in comparison to mouse and other mammalian orthologs, potentially with medically important phenotypic effects. Still, a gross level comparison might indicate that leptin has the same function in mice and humans.

A much more radical shift of function in chordates involves the emergence of antifreeze proteins in cold water fish. Antifreeze proteins have emerged in teleost fish nine different times from five different sources (reviewed in Cheng, 1998). Antifreeze glycoproteins emerged independently from a trypsinogen-type serine protease in the antarctic nototheniods and in the arctic cods. Type 1 antifreeze proteins evolved from an unknown origin in righteye flatfish and sculpins. Type 2 antifreeze proteins evolved from C-type lectin in Atlantic herring, rainbow smelt, and sea raven. Type 3 antifreeze proteins evolved from an unknown source in Zoarcoidei, like the wolf-fish. Finally, type 4 antifreeze proteins evolved from apolipoprotein in the long-horn sculpin. This remarkable degree of functional convergent evolution in teleost fish shows the flexibility of protein scaffolds to be biochemically shaped by selective pressures during neofunctionalization.

Evolution within the Biological Network

Ultimately, genes in a genome interact with each other to produce an organism. The emerging field of systems biology is focused on analyzing the connectivity of gene products through direct interaction, metabolism, and other mechanisms in connecting gene content to the encoded organism. The coevolution of genes in a genome is complex and involves many factors besides purely sequence, like transcription (see Wray et al., 2003), mRNA splicing (see Modrek and Lee, 2003), and others. Some properties of the process of network evolution are beginning to emerge in this developing synthesis. Most (but not all) diversity seems to originate through gene duplication (Babu and Teichmann, 2004). Genes duplicated through whole genome duplication may have been subject to different constraints from genes that were duplicated without their interacting partners. Evidence from yeast (preceding the chordate and plant whole genome duplications) indicates that evolution has evolved incrementally without the exact copying of subnetworks (Babu and Teichmann, 2004). Correspondingly, there is a high rate of interaction loss after duplication in yeast, but a much slower rate of evolution of new interactions (Wagner, 2001). However, most interactions that have been retained do come from genes that have been duplicated at similar times (Qin et al., 2003). Therefore, because of network effects, whole chromosome or genome duplication may be an especially powerful mechanism for genome divergence and the emergence of new functionality. Large scale duplication does appear to have played important roles in shaping the genome contents of both chordates and embryophytes.

Many processes have shaped the genome contents we see today in chordates and higher plants. Differences in genome content enable differential adaptation to environments and different organismal life strategies. As more genomes are sequenced from more species, our understanding of genomic biology at this level will only increase.

References

Allen KD. 2002. Assaying gene content in Arabidopsis. *Proc. Natl. Acad. Sci., USA* 99:9568-9572.

Andersson, JO and Roger AJ. 2002. Evolutionary analyses of the small subunit of glutamate synthase: Gene order conservation, gene fusions, and prokaryote-to-eukaryote lateral gene transfer. *Eukaryotic Cell* 1:304-310.

Aparicio S, Chapman J, Stupka E, Putnam N, Chia J et al. 2002. Whole-genome shotgun assemby and analysis of the genome of *Fugu rubripes. Science* 297:1301-1310.

Arvestad L, Berglund AC, Lagergren J, and Sennblad B. 2003. Bayesian Gene/Species Tree Reconciliation and Orthology Analysis Using MCMC. *Bioinformatics* 19:I7-I15.

Babu MM and Teichmann SA. 2004. Gene regulatory network growth by duplication. *Nature Genetics* 36:492-496.

Bateman A, Birney E, Cerruti L, Durbin R, Etwiller L et al. 2002. The pfam protein families database. *Nucleic Acids Res.* 30:276-80.

Benner SA, Trabesinger N, and Scheiber D. 1998. Post-genomic science: Converting primary sequence into physiological function. *Adv. Enzyme Regul.* 38:155-190.

Bergthorsson U, Adams KL, Thomason B, and Palmer JD. 2003. Widespread horizontal transfer of mitochondrial genes in flowering plants. *Nature* 424:197-201.

Bi S, Garilova O, Gong DW, Mason MM, and Reitman M. 1997. Identification of a placental enhancer for the human leptin gene. *J. Biol. Chem.* 272:30583-30588.

Boucher Y, and Doolittle WF. 2000. The role oflateral gene transfer in the evolution of isoprenoid biosynthesis pathways. *Mol. Microbiol.* 37:703-716.

Cheng CHC. 1998. Evolution of diverse antifreeze proteins. *Curr. Opin. Gen. Dev.* 8:715-720.

Cho Y, Qui YL, Kuhlman P, and Palmer JD. 1998. Explosive invasion of plant mitochondria by a group I intron. *Proc. Natl. Acad. Sci., USA* 95:14244-14249.

Clamp M, Andrews D, Barker D, Bevan G, Cameron G et al. 2003. Ensembl 2002: accommodating comparative genomics. *Nucleic Acids Res.* 31:38-42.

Clark AG, Glanowski S, Nielsen R, Thomas PD, Kejariwal A et al. 2003. Inferring nonneutral evolution from human-chimp-mouse orthologous gene trios. *Science* 302:1960-1963.

Davis RH, Morris DR, and Coffino P. 1992. Sequestered end products and enzyme regulation: The case of ornithine decarboxylase. *Microbiol. Rev.* 56:280-290.

Dehal P, Satou Y, Campbell RK, Chapman J, Degnan B et al. 2002. The draft genome of *Ciona intestinalis*: insights into chordate and vertebrate origins. *Science*, 298:2157-2167.

de Koning AP, Brinkman FSL, Jones SJM, and Keelings PJ. 2000. Lateral gene transfer and metabolic adaptation in the human parasite *Trichomonas vaginalis*. *Mol. Biol. Evol.* 17:1769-1773.

Doolittle WF. 1999. Phylogenetic classification and the universal tree. *Science* 284:2124-2128.

Duret L, Mouchiroud D, Gouy M. 1994. HOVERGEN: A database of homologous vertebrate genes. *Nucl. Acids Res.* 22:2360-2365.

Field J, Rosenthal B, and Samuelson J. 2000. Early lateral transfer of genes encoding malic enzyme, acetyl-CoA synthetase and alcohol dehydrogenases from anaerobic prokaryotes to *Entamoeba histolytica. Mol. Microbiol.* 38:446-455.

Fitch WM. 1970. Distinguishing homologous from analogous proteins. *Syst. Zool.* 19:99-113.

Force A, Lynch M, Pickett FB, Amores A, Yan YL, and Postlethwait J. 1999. Preservation of duplicate genes by complementary, degenerative mutations. *Genetics* 151:1531-1545.

Fukami-Kobayashi K, Schreiber DR, and Benner SA. 2003. Detecting compensatory covariation signals in protein evolution using reconstructed ancestral sequences. *J. Mol. Biol.* 319:729-743.

Gaucher EA, Gu X, Miyamoto MM, and Benner SA. 2002. Predicting functional divergence in protein evolution by site-specific rate shifts. *Trends Biochem. Sci.* 27:315-321.

Gaucher EA, Miyamoto MM, and Benner SA. 2003. Evolutionary, structural, and biochemical evidence for a new interaction site of the leptin obesity protein. *Genetics* 163:1549-1553.

Gilad Y, Man O, Pääbo S, and Lancet D. 2003. Human specific loss of olfactory receptor genes. *Proc. Natl. Acad. Sci., USA* 100:3324-3327.

Goff SA, Ricke D, Lan TH, Presting G, Wang R et al. 2002. A draft sequence of the rice genome (*Oryza sativa* L. ssp. *japonica*). *Science* 296:92-100.

Henze K, Horner DS, Suguri S, Moore DV, Sánchez LB, Müller M, and Embley TM. 2001. Unique phylogenetic relationships of glucokinase and glucosephosphate isomerase of the amitochondriate eukaryotes *Giardia intestinalis*, *Spironucleus barkhanus* and *Trichomonas vaginalis. Gene* 281:123-131.

Hiroike T, Higo J, Jingami H, and Toh H. 2000. Homology modeling of human leptin/leptin receptor complex. *Biochem. Biophys. Res. Comm.* 275:154-158.

Hokamp K, McLysaght A, and Wolfe KH. 2003. The 2R hypothesis and the human genome sequence. *J. Struct. Funct. Genomics* 3:95-110.

Holland LZ and Gibson-Brown JJ. The *Ciona intestinalis* genome: when the constraints are off. *Bioessays* 25:529-532.

Huang CY, Ayliff MA, and Timmis JN. 2003. Direct measurement of the transfer rate of chloroplast DNA into the nucleus. *Nature* 422:72-76.

Hughes AL and Friedman R. 2R or not 2R: testing hypotheses of genome duplication in early vertebrates. *J. Struct. Funct. Genomics* 3:85-93.

Intrieri MC and Buiatti M. 2001. The horizontal transfer of *Agrobacterium rhizogenes* genes and the evolution of the genus *Nicotiana. Mol. Phylogenet. Evol.* 20:100-110.

Jain R, Rivera MC, Moore JE, and Lake JA. 2003. Horizontal gene transfer accelerates genome innovation and evolution. *Mol. Biol. Evol.* 20:1598-1602.

Kapitonov VV and Jurka J. 1999. The long terminal repeat of an endogenous retrovirus induces alternative splicing and encodes an additional carboxy-terminal sequence in the human leptin receptor. *J. Mol. Evol.* 48:248-251.

Katju V and Lynch M. 2003. The structure and early evolution of recently arisen gene duplicates in the *Caenorhabditis elegans* genome. *Genetics* 165:1793:1803.

Koonin EV. 2003. Comparative genomics, minimal gene-sets and the last universal common ancestor. *Nat. Rev. Microbiol.* 1:127-136.

Kumar A, Taylor MA, Mad Arif SA, and Davies HV. 1996. Potato plants expressing antisense and sense S-adenosyl decarboxylase (SAMDC) transgenes show altered levels of polyamines and ethylene: antisense plants display abnormal phenotypes. *Plant J.* 9:147-158.

Kurland CG, Canback B, and Berg OG. 2003. Horizontal gene transfer: A critical view. *Proc. Natl. Acad. Sci., USA* 100:9658-9662.

Lander ES, Linton LM, Birren B, Nusbaum C, Zody MC et al. 2001. Initial sequencing and analysis of the human genome. *Nature* 409:860-921.

Lawrence JG and Hendrickson H. 2003. Lateral gene transfer: when will adolescence end? *Mol. Microbiol.* 50:739-749.

Lawrence JG and Ochman H. 1998. Molecular archeology of the *Escherichia coli* genome. *Proc. Natl. Acad. Sci., USA* 95: 9413-9417.

Letunic I, Copley RR, Schmidt S, Ciccarelli FD, Doerks T, Schultz J, Ponting CP, and Bork P. 2004. SMART 4.0: towards genomic data integration. *Nucleic Acids Res.* 32:D142-D144.

Leveugle M, Prat K, Popovici C, Birnbaum D, and Coulier F. 2004. Phylogenetic analysis of *Ciona intestinalis* gene superfamilies supports the hypothesis of successive gene expansions. *J. Mol. Evol.* 58:168-181.

Liberles DA, Schreiber DR, Govindarajan S, Chamberlin SG, and Benner SA. 2001. The Adaptive Evolution Database (TAED). *Genome Biol.* 2(8):research0028.1-research0028.6.

Lister DL, Bateman JM, Purton S, and Howe CJ. 2003. DNA transfer from chloroplast to nucleus is much rarer in *Chlamydomonas* than in tobacco. *Gene* 316:33-38.

Lynch M and Conery JS. 2000. The evolutionary fate and consequences of duplicate genes. *Science* 290:1151-1155.

Martin W. 2003. Gene transfer from organelles to the nucleus: Frequent and in big chunks. *Proc. Natl. Acad. Sci., USA* 100:8612-8614.

Meyerowitz EM. 2002. Plants compared to animals: The broadest comparative study of development. *Science* 295:1482-1485.

Modrek B and Lee CJ. 2003. Alternative splicing in the human, mouse, and rat genomes is associated with an increased frequency of exon creation and/or loss. *Nature Genetics* 34:177-180.

Nicolau KC, Yang Z, Liu JJ, Ueno H, Nantermet PG et al. 1994. The total synthesis of taxol. *Nature* 367:630-634.

Ochman H, Lawrence JG, and Groisman EA. 2000. Lateral gene transfer and the nature of bacterial innovation. *Nature* 405:299-304.

Ohno S. 1970. *Evolution by gene duplication*. New York: Springer-Verlag.

Ota R and Penny D. 2003. Estimating changes in mutational mechanisms of evolution. *J. Mol. Evol.* 57:S233-S240.

Pendleton JW, Nagai BK, Murtha MT, and Ruddle FH. 1993. Expansion of the hox gene family and the evolution of chordates. *Proc. Natl. Acad. Sci., USA* 90:6300-6304.

Podlaha O and Zhang J. 2003. Positive selection on protein-length in the evolution of a primate sperm ion channel. *Proc. Natl. Acad. Sci., USA* 100:12241-12246.

Pollock DD and Taylor WR. 1997. Effectiveness of correlation analysis in identifying protein residues undergoing correlated evolution. *Protein Eng.* 10:647-657.

Pollock DD, Taylor WR, and Goldman N. 1999. Coevolving protein residues: maximum likelihood identification and relationship to structure. *J. Mol. Biol.* 287:187-198.

Pruess M, Fleischmann W, Kanapin A, Karavidopoulou Y, Kersey P et al. 2003. The proteome analysis database: a tool for the in silico analysis of whole proteomes. *Nucleic Acids Res*, 31:414-417.

Qin H, Lu HHS, Wu WB, and Li WH. 2003. Evolution of the yeast protein inteaction network. *Proc. Natl. Acad. Sci., USA* 100:12820-12824.

Rat Genome Sequencing Project Consortium. 2004. Genome sequence of the brown Norway rat yields insights into mammalian evolution. *Nature* 428:493-521.

Salzberg SL, White O, Peterson J, and Eisen JA. 2001. Microbial genes in the human genome: Lateral transfer or gene loss? *Science* 292:1903-1906.

Siltberg J and Liberles, DA. 2002. A simple covarion-based approach to analyse nucleotide substitution rates. *J. Evol. Biol.* 15:588-594.

Sonnhammer EL and Koonin EV. 2002. Orthology, paralogy and proposed classification for paralog subtypes. *Trends Genet.* 18:619-620.

Soyer OS, Dimmic MW, Neubig RR, and Goldstein RA. 2003. Dimerization in aminergic G-protein-coupled receptors: Application of a hidden-site class model of evolution. *Biochem.* 42:14522-14531.

Spagnuolo A, Ristoratore F, Gregorio DA, Aniello F, Branno M, Lauro DR. 2003. Unusual number and genomic organization of hox genes in the tunicate *Ciona intestinalis*. *Gene*, 309:71-79.

Stanhope MJ, Lupas A, Italia MJ, Koretke KK, Volker C, and Brown JR. 2001. Phylogenetic analyses do not support horizontal gene transfer from bacteria to vertebrates. *Nature* 411:940-944.

Stegeman S, Hartmann S, Ruf S, and Bock R. 2003. High-frequency gene transfer from the chloroplast genome to the nucleus. *Proc. Natl. Acad. Sci., USA* 100:8828-8833.

Strobel GA, Stierle A, Stierle D, and Hess WH. 1993. T*axomyces andreanae* a proposed new taxon for a bulbilliferous hyphomycete associated with Pacific yew. *Mycotaxon* 47:71-78.

Strobel GA. 2003. Endophytes as sources of bioactive products. Micorbes Infect. 5:535-544.

Suguri S, Henze K, Sánchez LB, Moore DV, Müller M. 2001. Archaebacterial relationships of the phosphoenolpyruvate carboxykinase gene reveal mosaicism of *Giardia intestinalis* core metabolism. *J. Eukaryot. Microbiol.* 48:493-497.

Tatusov RL, Fedorova ND, Jackson JD, Jacobs AR, Kiryutin B et al. 2003. The cog database: an updated version includes eukaryotes. *BMC Bioinformatics* 4:41.

The Arabidopsis Genome Initiative. 2000. Analysis of the genome sequence of the flowering plant *Arabidopsis thaliana*. *Nature* 408:796-815.

Torrents D, Suyama M, Zdobnov E, and Bork P. 2003. Genome-wide survey of human pseudogenes. *Genome Res.* 13:2559-2567.

Venter JC, Adams MD, Myers EW, Li PW, Mural RJ et al. 2001. The sequence of the human genome. *Science* 291:1304.

Wagner A. 2001. The yeast protein interaction network evolves rapidly and contains few redundant duplicate genes. *Mol. Biol. Evol.* 18:1283-1292.

Wagner GP, Amemiya C, and Ruddle F. 2003. Hox cluster duplications and the opportunity for evolutionary novelties. *Proc. Natl. Acad. Sci., USA* 100:14603-14606.

Walters DR. 2003. Polyamines and plant disease. *Phytochemistry* 64: 97-107.

Waterston RH, Lindblad-Toh K, Birney E, Rogers J, Abril JF et al. 2002. Initial sequencing and comparative analysis of the mouse genome. *Nature* 420:520-562.

Watson MB, Emory KK, Piatak RM, and Malmberg L. 1998. Arginine decarboxylase (polyamine synthesis) mutants of *Arabidopsis thaliana* exhibit altered root growth. *Plant J.* 13: 231-239.

White FF, Garfinkel DJ, Huffman GA, Gordon MP, and Nester EW. 1983. Sequence homologous to *Agrobacterium rhizogenes* T-DNA in the genome of uninfected plants. *Nature* 301:348-350.

Whiting PJ, Bonnert TP, McKernan RM, Farrar S, Bourdelles LB et al. 1999. Molecular and functional diversity of the expanding receptor gene family. *Ann. N.Y. Acad. Sci.* 868:645-653.

Wray GA, Hahn MW, Abouheif E, Balhoff JP, Pizer M, Rockman MV, and Romano LA. 2003. The evolution of transcriptional regulation in eukaryotes. *Mol. Biol. Evol.* 20:1377-1419.

Won H and Renner SS. 2003 Horizontal gene transfer from flowering plants to *Gnetum*. *Proc. Natl. Acad. Sci., USA* 100:10824-10829.

Yu J, Hu S, Wang J, Wong GK, Li S, et al. 2002. A draft sequence of the rice genome (*Oryza sativa* L. ssp. *indica*). *Science* 296:79-92.

Zhang J. 2003. Evolution by gene duplication: an update. *Trends Ecol. Evol.* 18:292-298.

Zhang Z, Harrison PM, Liu Y, and Gerstein M. 2003. Millions of years of evolution preserved: a comprehensive catalog of the processed pseudogenes in the human genome. *Genome Res.* 13:2541-2558.

In: Trends in Bioinformatics Research   ISBN 1-59454-739-4
Editor: Peter V. Yan, pp. 119-141   © 2005 Nova Science Publishers, Inc.

Chapter V

Open Source, Open Formats, Open Data – Democratizing Bioinformatics Research

*Mads Wichmann Matthiessen**
Department of Medical Gastroenterology C112,
Herlev University Hospital, 2730 Herlev, Denmark

Abstract

Bioinformatics research has developed at a rapid pace throughout the last decade. While the applications available at the end of the last century were mostly developed as tools for assisting regular molecular biologists or epidemiologist, more recently, the sequencing of several genomes, the large roll out of DNA microarray analysis equipment, and development of high throughput screening methods have required that software is developed to assist in bioinformatics analysis of the tremendous amounts of data produced by these methods. For the most part, these highly specialized software packages have been developed commercially and have - only been available at a premium cost. However, maturation of the laboratory technologies as well as the introduction and proliferation of open source software development in most categories of software (microarray expression analysis, genome analysis, office applications, graphics manipulation and advanced statistical analysis) has leveled the playing field in such a way that bioinformatics research is now available to anyone with a contemporary computer and an Internet connection. The parallel development of open data formats (most importantly XML) has had the similarly important implication that it is now possible to use different software applications to analyse the same data natively, such that firstly,

*Correspondence: Department of Medical Gastroenterology C112, Herlev University Hospital, 2730 Herlev, Denmark. E-mail: ns@madswichmann.dk, website: www.madswichmann.dk

applications compete on their quality and not on monopoly, and secondly, that the data is independent of the survival of specific software companies.

In this chapter, the advantages of open formats and open source software are described and relevant software for creating biocomputing platforms and networks are suggested.

1   Introduction

Bioinformatics research has until recently been possible mostly in well funded organizations. Many public institutions, such as hospitals, universities, schools and laboratories, have had limited resources for purchasing expensive proprietary biology analysis software and even office and productivity applications. This has previously been due to the high cost of bioanalytical software and the specialized hardware (high powered unix servers) that is necessary to run this software, effectively making professional bioinformatics systems only available for use in private companies or well-funded organizations. Even standard office and productivity software, graphics manipulation and reference management software is very costly and is usually prioritized very low in institutions with insufficient software budgets. This has had the unfortunate effect, that biological researchers have not been able to utilize the full power of computers to design and analyse experiments. Although most researchers have had some software available, it is frequently out-dated and has seen limited integration into the research process restricting the benefits of contemporary powerful computers into biological research.

With the recent international incorporation of the Internet into virtually all fields of science and particularly within the biological and medical research communities, a substantial number of professional tools have been developed and released for free. Additionally, maturation and a significant number of advances of open-source software extending from the operating system to desktop applications in combination with the availability of inexpensive and high powered desktop computers, have eliminated the requirements for customized computing platforms running proprietary and expensive office and bioinformatics software. Currently, it is possible to create highly capable and fully professional computer systems and networks that, independent of software budgets, allows for fully functional and advanced bioinformatics workstations to be assembled from low-end computers with an Internet connection.

In this chapter, the advantages of open formats and open source software are described and relevant software for creating biocomputing platforms and networks are suggested. A number of open source applications selected from different software categories (productivity/office applications, reference management and biocomputing software) of relevance both to traditional and bioinformatics researchers will be described. All of the software mentioned here is free and most of the applications can be run on any major operating system.

1.1 Bioinformatics Research

Computational biology or bioinformatics research are loosely defined terms that describe the integration and use of computer analysis into biological and medical research and development. Development of tools and methods in bioinformatics research have progressed significantly over the last decade, particularly as a positive side effect of the necessity for these tools in the large genome sequencing projects. Following the completion of genomic sequencing, the need to understand and rapidly assign meaning and function to the excessive amounts of primary sequence data has only furthered the advancements of bioinformatics software.

1.1.1 Systems Biology

The traditional research method, that seeks to examine isolated cause and effect interactions, have not been able to deliver sufficient understanding of complicated signaling networks, such as those involved in major diseases, for instance diabetes and inflammatory diseases. The complexity of interacting cellular components in pathways of signaling and metabolism or even cell to cell communication, represents a truly formidable task that requires new approaches [1]. The Systems Biology approach seeks to analyze biological information at multiple levels, with the aim to construct quantitative models for entire cells or even organisms [2]. A cellular system is more than the sum of its components - namely a set of relationships between the parts that make up the system. The ultimate goal is to encompass all processes including cellular metabolism, gene regulation and signal transduction. This will pave the way for *in silico* modeling of cell physiology, organ function and allow disease behavior to be fully understood [1, 3].

New technologies including DNA arrays, automated RT-PCR, two-dimensional gel electrophoresis and antibody arrays, allows the determination of RNA and protein expression profiles in great detail. These achievements provide, in principle, the entire spectrum of analytical elements needed to fully understand the integrated function of the living cell. Major challenges, however, still remain before the full advantage can be gained from this vast amount of information. In order to fully describe the function of the cell, all the interactions between the many components at different levels (DNA, RNA, protein, metabolites) must be well described and understood. A similarly important task is the storing and integration of the data in an intuitive and efficient manner and development of powerful data mining methods and tools to fully take advantage of the generated data. An integrated bioinformatics approach for analyzing the genes, single nucleotide polymorphisms, protein structure, molecular interactions, post transcriptional and translational modifications, protein and mRNA degradation, activation and sorting will be fundamental to modern biomedical research in general.

The goal of these many different aspects of bioinformatics research is to corroborate research by extracting knowledge from high throughput results and by predicting complex systems both within and between cells. Bioinformatics is integral to the evolution of primary sequence data into valuable functional databases that contain accumulated biological knowledge from a plethora of resources.

1.1.2   The Challenge: Integrating the Data with the Tools

Bioinformatics resources have been developed in very disparate environments (massively funded government efforts, corporate development and hobby-projects). Even more, the quality of the resources vary greatly. Therefore, one of the major challenges of harvesting the full potential of bioinformatics resources (tools and data), is the integration and curation of widely different data formats and application interfaces. Currently, after thoroughly browsing through databases either manually or by using tools to gather relevant data, researchers will themselves have to do most of the integration between different resources. To find answers to advanced bioinformatics queries, this is usually done either on their own computer or on a piece of paper. Obviously, this compounds a number of issues, such as manual errors, time consumption and data fatigue, leading to distorted conclusions, lost opportunity and less than optimal productivity. Particularly, the high rate of creation of relevant databases [4, 5] with different interfaces and data structures, has only furthered the need for data and tool integration and standardization.

1.1.3 The Solution: Standards

The solution to this problem, standardized data formats, is in theory simple, yet in practice difficult to achieve [6]. Firstly, because databases may not instantly match common standards and secondly, because the effort needed to transform data and tools to conform might be less than trivial and may break compatibility with software developed by other parties. Fortunately, a number of community efforts are directed at unifying data formats, storage and application interfaces to develop this much needed integration of the high number of orphaned but valuable resources.

For instance, the distributed annotation system (DAS) is a client-server system in which a single client integrates information from multiple servers [7]. It allows a single machine to gather genome annotation information through multiple remote servers and integrate the information so it can be displayed as a unified view of the currently available information. DAS is used for large genome projects such as WormBase (http://www.wormbase.org/) and Ensembl (http://www.ensembl.org/). Furthermore, a number of client applications that use this common standard have been developed for efficient handling of specific tasks.

Similar to DAS, BioMOBY is an open source research project which aims to generate an architecture for the discovery and distribution of biological data through web services [8]. The data and services are decentralised, but the availability of these resources, and the instructions for interacting with them, are registered in a central location called a MOBY Central.

Another effort is the Gene ontology consortium (http://www.geneontology. org/) whose goal it is to apply defined terms to describe gene product attributes and a standardized data format to gene and protein information, while enabling dynamic updating of the database as new information is made available [9]. The Gene ontology resource is providing a valuable database of integrated information from a variety of sources, which has proven to be a valuable tool for quickly assembling functional data on genes found to be of interest from high throughput methods, such as DNA microarray experiments.

A different approach, but one that accompanies the projects mentioned above are extensions to programming languages that are developed to access and further integration of databases and tools. In particular, BioPerl, BioPython and BioJava are worth mentioning and will be discussed in more detail below.

Most of these modern resources are communicating through globally adopted industry standards, such as Universal Data Discovery and Integration (UDDI), simple object access protocol (SOAP) transaction and eXtensible Markup Language (XML) data.

1.2   Open Source Software

Open-source software is being developed with the programming code freely available for anyone to obtain, use and develop further and is intended to be disseminated as widely as possible to have as many eyes on the source code as possible. In principle, this leads to strong peer-reviewing of the programming code, because problems and issues that were not thought of or discovered by the authors of the software can be addressed openly by other interested parties. With proper maintenance of the open source projects, secure and stable applications of very high quality can be developed. In some projects thousands of participants, ranging from teenage amateurs to software professionals, are involved in the development of the software.

Usually, the rapid development of open source software quickly delivers security and bug fixes, new features and enhancements. This is both an advantage and a disadvantage. For the casual user of the software, new features can be entertaining and something that the enthusiast are looking for, however, in a professional and production environment there usually is a requirement for software stability and reliability. Fortunately, the larger open source projects usually maintain two parallel lines of each product (branches). One branch is commonly termed "stable" and the other "development". The "stable" releases are for the most part only developed to incorporate bug and security fixes, whereas the "development" branch is receiving all enhancements to the product as well as being used for experimentation and new features. For any serious use, it is recommended that one uses the stable branch, but for most software it is possible that both branches can be installed and co-exist on the same machine, enabling the user to experience and take advantage of new and advanced features and familiarize one with the next "stable" version prior to its release.

The trade-off when using open source software instead of commercial solutions is convenience and user-friendliness for variety. But fortunately, recent progress in mainstream open source software development (OpenOffice, The GNOME and KDE desktop environments etc.) has been focused on the user experience and has rectified lacking ease-of-use to increase the appeal of the applications.

1.3   Open Licenses

The authors of open source programming code may want to retain a degree of control of the source code and for this, a multitude of license agreements have been developed. A large number of which are available from The Free Software Foundation (http://www.fsf.org). These licenses differ mostly by the way they require the licensee (the persons using the software) to handle the derivative programming code. Some allow derived software to be sold commercially as closed compiled programs, whereas other licenses require that the entire source is released to the public. The most well known open source license is the Gnu is not unix (GNU) general public license (GPL), which is very open and absolutely states that the derived work must be given back to the community. While other licenses are more pragmatic in their approach to licensing and some even allow derived work to be closed source and sold commercially.

Apart from general copyright laws, open data is not yet as frequently protected by licenses specific for data as is open source software. However, a number of licenses have been developed by Creative Commons (http://creativecommons.org/) that in similar ways to source code licenses de-scribe levels of acknowledgment and how the data can be copied, used and transformed. Again many of these licenses require that the data is returned in an open format to the public.

1.4   Open Formats

To truly take advantage of the plethora of tools and databases available from the open community, data formats also need to be open and well described. A num-ber of international bodies (IEEE, W3C etc) work towards creating a consensus between interested developers of both data and software to reach agreement on common data and file formats. While this may seem like the optimal approach, it sometimes has the disadvantage of exceedingly slow progress and in some instances data formats need to be developed rapidly. In the latter situation, the format should nevertheless still be well described and open. Open data formats binds software and data together independently of whom have produced either and lets users select software on the basis of its merit, cost and quality. Secondly, open data-formats makes it readily possible to convert data from one format to another. Keeping the data-format closed is in some cases a way to keep the cus-tomers tied into proprietary and costly software. However, the greatest threat from closed formats is that the developers cease to exist and the format is lost, such that unique and invaluable databases and files stored for years in public and corporate archives may be permanently lost, since no software is available to access and process the data.

In order to facilitate data comparison, exchange and verification within research communities, the data need to be described in a reliable and consistent manner. Specific to the field of bioinformatics research, a number of standards are being developed. The Proteomics Standards Initiative (http://psidev. sourceforge.net/) is working towards defining community standards for data representation, comparison and verification from proteomics experiments and mass spectrometry. The Minimal Information About a Proteomics Experiment (MIAPE) is attempting a refined data model and a repository for published proteomics data and the Minimal Information for the Annotation of a Microarray Experiment (MIAME) and Microarray Gene Expression (MAGE-ML) standards are designed to describe and communicate information about DNA microarray based experiments [10].

2 The Software - Setting Up Bioinformatics Workstations

In the following, a number of open-source and free alternatives to commercial software applications are presented. In cases where nothing else is mentioned, the software is available for common platforms (Linux, Apple and Microsoft Windows) and in many cases the software is pre-installed on Linux systems.

2.1 Office and Productivity Packages

2.1.1 Office Software

Advanced cross platform productivity suites released as open sources have recently matured and are now available with a full complement of any application an office will ever require. For instance the OpenOffice.org package (http://www.openoffice.org/) includes word processing-, spreadsheet-, reference management-, database-, presentation-, formula editing- and drawing-software. It is even capable of importing and exporting to many other file formats, such as Microsoft Office and WordPerfect. AbiWord (http://www.abisource.com/) is a light-weight, but fully competent and advanced word processor that features spell-checking, a thesaurus and limited reference management. As an alternative for Linux-users, KOffice (http://www.koffice.org/) is a smaller suite that delivers the needed office-applications.

A popular way to distribute read-only versions of documents (text as well as graphics) is to use the platform-independent Adobe Acrobat portable document format files (PDF-files). These files can be produced easily through OpenOffice.org or more advanced through the use of the Ghostscript package (http://www.cs.wisc.edu/ ghost/) that converts almost any file format into the PDF format via an intermediate postscript file. In Windows, the incredibly uncomplicated PDFcreator (https://sourceforge.net/projects/pdfcreator/), which is build on Ghostscript, simply installs as a printer driver and lets one print directly to a PDF file from any application.

For the adventurous, LaTeX (For Mac: http://www.esm.psu.edu/mac-tex/, and for Windows: http://www.miktex.org/) is a completely professional layout system that can produce almost any open file format (PDF, postscript, HTML and text-files) and incorporates the BibTeX reference management software (see below). It is text based, but graphical user interfaces are available for those so inclined. For instance, TeXnicCenter for Windows (Fig. 1) (http://www.texniccenter.org) is a small but highly functional and configurable editor including a spellchecker and support for the BibTex reference management format (see below). Available as a cross-platform application, LYX is a 'What you see is what you mean' (WYSIWYM) LaTeX-editor (Fig. 2) (http://www.lyx.org/), similar to regular word processing software, such as Word-Perfect and Microsoft Word.

2.1.2 Reference Management

Reference management is an integral part of most researchers work. As previously mentioned, both OpenOffice.Org and Abiword contain limited reference management functionality. JabRef (http://jabref.sourceforge.net/) is a specialized reference management tool, which natively uses the BibTeX reference format (Fig. 3). It is able to retrieve records directly from Medline and import other reference formats, such as Reference Manager, Scifinder, INSPEC and Ovid.

2.1.3 Project and Data Management

Collaborating with other researchers sometimes requires a certain degree of formalized project management. For smaller projects, a simple Gantt chart may be sufficient to outline the involved participants, their responsibilities, time allocation and work load and for this, the Gantt-project is well suited (http://ganttproject.sourceforge.net/) (Fig. 4).

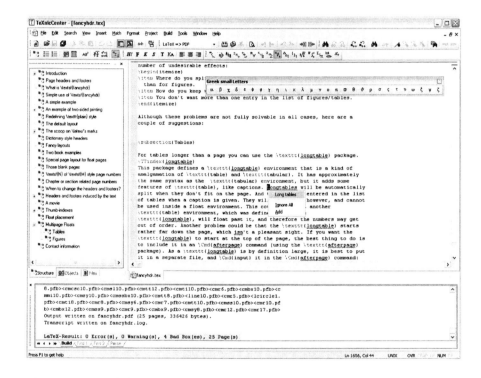

Fig. 1: LaTeX editing in an integrated development editor - TeXnicCenter. TeXnicCenter is a small but highly functional and configurable editor for LaTeX files. It includes a spellchecker and support for the BibTeX reference format.

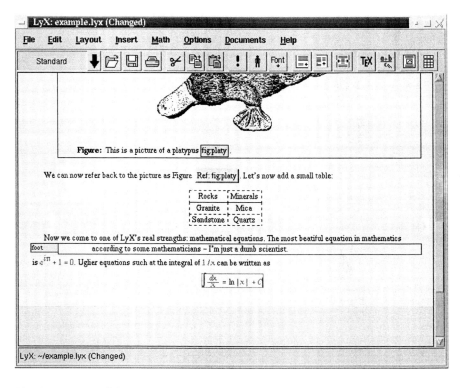

Fig. 2: LaTeX editing with a graphical user interface - LYX.
LYX is a cross-platform "'What you see is what you mean'" (WYSIWYM) LaTeX-editor similar to regular word processing software.

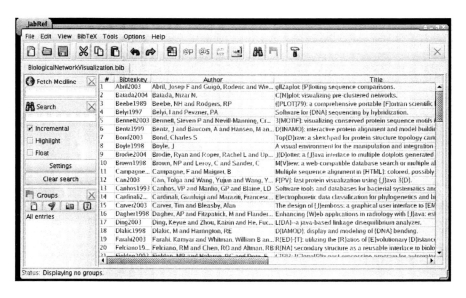

Fig. 3: Reference Management - JabRef.

JabRef is a reference management tool, which natively uses the BibTeX reference format. It is able to retrieve records directly from Medline and import other reference formats, such as Reference Manager, Scifinder, INSPEC and Ovid.

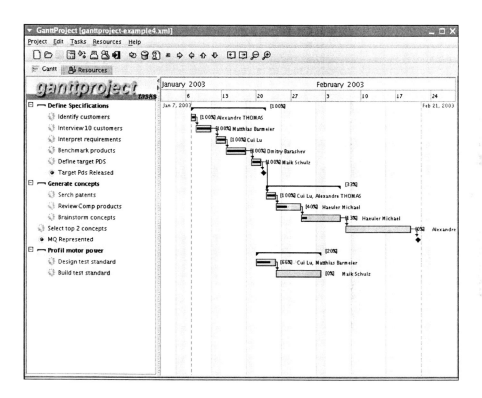

Fig. 4: Project management - The Gantt-project.

The Gantt-project manages Gantt charts that outlines the involved participants, their responsibilities, time allocation and work load. It is written in Java and therefore is available across many different platforms.

For larger projects containing thousands of data files and documents, advanced tools developed to maintain software projects are available from the open source community and are readily available for managing both projects and data (see section 2.4).

2.1.4   Statistical Software

The R-project (http://www.r-project.org/), derived from the S-language, is a script based statistical environment and is particularly suited for bioinformatics research due to the extension packages that are available for DNA microarray analysis. These packages support all common DNA microarray data-formats (GenePixPro, Spotfinder, Affymetrix) and allow the researcher to rapidly process multiple experiments with advanced control over the analysis parameters.

A completely different approach to statistical analysis is available from the Visual Statistics System (ViSta) (http://forrest.psych.unc.edu/research/), which uses an unconventional graphical user interface to achieve a more visual approach to understanding and planning the statistical analysis workflow needed in a project, similar to what is found in the commercially available LabView program (Fig. 5).

2.1.5   Photo and Image Manipulation

Publication grade illustrations can be created in OpenOffice.org or KOffice. Photos, Illustrations and images can then be further manipulated in the Gimp (Fig. 6) (http://developer.gimp.org/ index.html), which is a versatile and advanced photo-editing program that parallels Adobe Photoshop both in the number and complexity of functions and is even compatible with Photoshop filter plug-ins, giving access to thousands of additional free image manipulation tools.

A set of command-line utilities, collectively named ImageMagick (http://www.imagemagick.org/), can resize, rotate and is able to convert almost any existing image format. It is optimized for processing of multiple files at a time and is particularly useful in combination with other script based utilities. For instance, a programming interface to ImageMagick has been developed for the Perl programming language (http://perl.org).

2.1.6   Internet Utilities

Most operating systems include basic tools for Internet usage, but it is worth the effort to install independent and standards compliant alternatives. The Mozilla

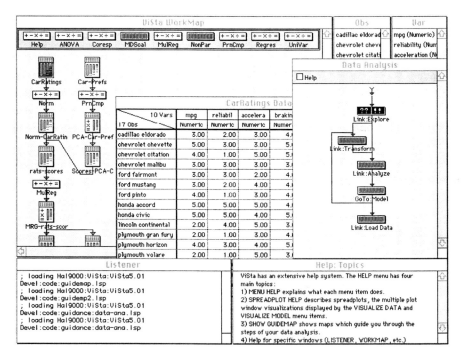

Fig. 5: Statistical software - ViSta.

A completely different approach to statistical analysis is available from the The Visual Statistics System (ViSta). ViSta uses a graphical user interface to achieve a more visual approach to understanding and planning the statistical analysis workflow for a project.

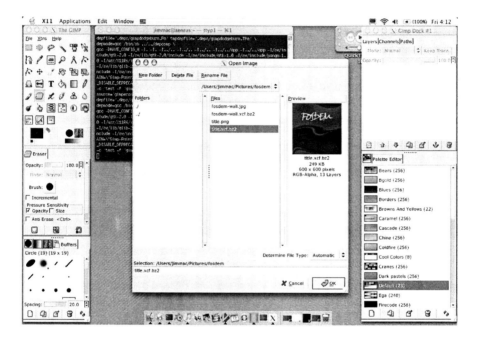

Fig. 6: Image editing - The Gimp.

The Gimp can be used for advanced image editing, supports Adobe Photoshop filter plug-ins and is compatible with most image formats. A number of dialog-boxes and palettes control various settings. FilmGimp, a descendent of the Gimp-project, even handles movie files.

organization (http://mozilla.org) has developed a number of cross platform tools. For Internet browsing, Mozilla Firefox (http://www.mozilla.org/products/firefox/) is excellent and can access PubMed through a plug-in based search function. Mozilla Thunderbird is an advanced email client, which includes a Bayesian spam filter (http://www.mozilla.org/mailnews/spam.html), which effectively eliminates 99 % of email spam after initial training. Both OpenOffice.org and Mozilla include HTML/Web page editing software, which makes it straightforward to maintain a website if one has that possibility. Mozilla also includes Chatzilla, an Internet relay chat (IRC) program. For file transfer protocol (FTP) operations, the FileZilla project (http://filezilla.sourceforge.net) has developed both client and server software. Practically, all the instant messaging (IM) networks can be accessed through Gaim (http://gaim.sourceforge.net/) or Trillian (http://www.trillian.cc/).

2.2   Computational Biology and Bioinformatics Tools

Simple computational manipulation of DNA, RNA and protein is highly available through Internet portals, that make it possible to submit DNA, RNA or protein sequences for a number of routine tasks such as sequence alignments, contig assembling, translation, exon/intron identification, phylogenic clustering, restriction enzyme digestion, plasmid maps and homology searching. Although these tools are great for analysis and preparation of experiments and usually support the same data-formats, they do not always integrate well and can be difficult to use for high throughput computations.

2.2.1   Molecular Biology Tools

The Baylor College of Medicine BCM Search Launcher [11] has an extensive set of tools available and also provides a small program for downloading, which can be used to submit multiple sequences for analysis. The SEquence analysis using WEb Resources site (SeWeR), is an attractive Internet portal that allows for integration of outside tools through a customization feature [12] (http://iubio.bio.indiana.edu/webapps/SeWeR/). It is even possible to setup and alter SeWeR locally through a download on the website. The Biology Workbench, co-developed by University of Illinois and UC San Diego [13], is another Internet portal, which supplies a large array of biocomputing tools and additionally provides an online workspace for saving sequences, files and results on the web server for future use. It is possible to prepare oligo DNA primers for polymerase chain reactions (PCR) with the Primer3 tool, which electronically attempts to eliminate as many pitfalls of PCR as possible (primer-dimers and self-complementarity), and allows for specification of experimental variables, for example primer degeneracy, melting temperature and ion concentration of buffers.

2.2.2   Structural Biology

Three dimensional protein structures, for example from the Protein Data Bank [14], can be visualized and manipulated (mutation of amino acids, twisting and turning of side chains and truncation of the protein chain) with the Swiss-PdbViewer [15], which can export to the Persistence of Vision Raytracer (POV-Ray), that produces spectacular visual representations of three dimensional protein models.

Visual Molecular Dynamics (VMD)(http://www.ks.uiuc.edu/Research/vmd/) is a molecular visualization program for displaying, animating, and analyzing large biomolecules using 3-D graphics and has built-in scripting for automating tasks.

If one wants to venture into protein homology modeling, Expasy offers this over the Internet via the Swiss-Model website that walks the researcher through the process. Secondary structure predictions of proteins is available from 3D-PSSM [16] and RNA and DNA can be folded and visualized through Zuker and Turners mFold server [17, 18].

2.2.3   Databases and Tools Relevant to Bioinformatics Research

Major molecular sequence data repositories are found at the US National Center for Biotechnological Information (NCBI) Genbank (http://www.ncbi.nih.gov/entrez/query.fcgi) and the European Molecular Biology Laboratory (EMBL) (http://www.ebi.ac.uk/embl/).   Protein structures can be found at the Research Collaboratory for Structural Bioinformatics - Protein Data Bank (http://www.rcsb.org/pdb/) and two resources that have made the numerous genomic sequence projects easily accessible are Ensembl (http://www.ensembl.org) and the Genome browser (http://genome.ucsc.edu).

Parallel to the increasing production of data from high throughput methods, bioinformatics research has developed from simply storing primary sequence data, to analysing and integrating distributed biological resources in order to describe complex cellular networks. This has led to a proliferation of functional databases and tools for gene prediction, comparative genomics, gene expression, metabolic pathways, protein-protein interactions etc. To mention a few, Resourcerer (Tsai, 2001), Genmapp (http://www.genmapp.org) and Pathway processor (Grosu et al., 2002) can map genes onto metabolic and regulatory pathways and provide organization of expression profiles.

Advances in biological software development over the last decades have led to a large amount of high quality applications developed both by the commercial and the open-source software community and whereas articles for a specific biomedical topic can be easily found through NCBI PubMed (http://pubmed. gov), it is far from trivial to find a software tool or a relevant database for a specific bioinformatics task, particularly for investigators with little experience in the field of bioinformatics..

However, a few searchable databases of biocomputing tools are available, such as The Biomedical Software and Database Search Engine (http://BioWare DB.org) [5]. With more than 3.800 records, BioWareDB, attempts to gather the largest possible number of entries of software and databases relevant to biological and medical researchers in an easily searchable index of validated entries to current and available biomedical computing resources. Additionally, the Structural Biology Software Database (http://www.ks.uiuc.edu/Development/ biosoftdb/) is available for researchers specializing in structural biology.

Furthermore, a number of software repositories are available for scientific open source software development (for example Sourceforge.net and bioinformatics.org) and a few specialized journals (i.e. The Nucleic Acid Research Database Issue [4] and The Bioinformatics Journal) have dedicated themselves to promoting the use and development of biocomputing tools and databases.

2.3   GNU/Linux

The free and highly successful operating system, GNU/Linux, is the progenitor of open source software (for background information on GNU/Linux visit http://www.linux.org/). Apart from the software mentioned above, GNU/Linux offers advanced options, such as multi computer clustering (for higher processing power) and a large number of software development tools and specialist programming tools. BioKnoppix, a bioinformatics linux distribution, is even available and is able to be booted directly from CD-ROM without the requirement for a hard disk, making it ideal for demonstration, education or bioinformatics on the go. GNU/Linux is available for almost any contemporary computer and thousands of free scientific programs for this operating system can currently be downloaded freely from the Internet.

2.4   Community Tools

A large number of community tools that enable researchers separated by distance to contribute to a common project are available. Most of these tools require a central webserver, which must be permanently connected to the Internet for optimal use.

Similar to the previously mentioned BioDAS and BioMOBY, the widely used Concurrent Versioning System (CVS) (http://www.cvshome.org/), can be used to develop databases in a revision and version controlled and collaborative fashion, such that it is always possible to backtrack and reverse changes if they should prove problematic. Secondly, the data can be entered by researchers at different geographic locales accessing a central repository through the Internet. CVS furthermore makes it possible to outline the history of changes of an object in the CVS repository.

To control issues and problems that need to be resolved, "bug"-tracking software, such as Bugzilla (http://www.bugzilla.org/) can be used to assign dependencies, responsibility, limitations and communication paths between involved researchers.

Community discussions on topics of relevance, can be had through bulletin board systems such as phpBB (http://www.phpbb.com/), which feature both open and closed discussion groups and can be access controlled.

Community knowledge databases are easy to setup, for instance by using the editable encyclopedia system, wikipedia (http://en.wikipedia.org/wiki/Wiki), researchers can share knowledge through a searchable and easily editable web interface.

2.5   Bioinformatics Programming Tools

A common feature of the following bioinformatics programming tools is that they are well suited for communication through the command-line interface. Although this initially might be a challenge to some, it is in fact a great advantage because it glues the output from different programs together by a common interface.

A hugely successful effort has been made by international open source collaboration by extending the Perl, Java and Python programming languages with bioinformatics extensions. These are called Bioperl, BioJava and Biopython and are available through the Open Bioinformatics Foundation (http://open-bio.org/), complete with source code and documentation. These extensions provide comprehensive libraries of modules that are available for managing and manipulating biomedical data. In combination with the powerful native data-handling routines of these languages, the extensions have enabled the much sought after integration of many databases and tools. These languages with extensions are available both as stand alone and server side tools and have made possible quite complex bioinformatics tasks with very limited programming experience. For instance, BioPerl, can tap directly into large public databanks, such as NCBI GenBank and rapidly retrieve and process thousands of sequences for motifs and then send the sequences of interest on to other databases or online tools for further processing with only a few lines of programming code. Most of the tools developed with these programming languages can be adapted for web-servers.

2.6   Networks, Grids and Distributed Computing

Hardware requirements have previously been a stumbling block for many users, but the processing power of modern computers has greatly outperformed the requirements of most software. Obviously, more powerful computer systems will increase the execution speed of programs, particularly when it comes to calculations of intensive tasks. However, advancing the computer power beyond a single PC, can be necessary to accomplish large computing projects that require extensive processing power. This, however, does not necessarily involve expensive hardware or advanced training. Projects, such as OpenMosix and the related KlusterKnoppix, delivers cluster computing through the simplest setup: you simply boot the computers you want included in a cluster from a CD-ROM, instantly turning them into peers in a distributed computing cluster.

For more advanced clustering, the DataGrid project can be used to make high end computing networks with processing power that have previously been restricted to military or physics research [19]. To make truly professional clusters, a Beowulf cluster can be set up, although this mechanism for clustering requires a substantial effort by the personnel involved in the setup and maintenance.

3   Conclusion

Availability and maturation of open source and free software have reached a critical point. It is presently possible to create highly capable and stable biocomputing systems with nothing more than the cost of low-budget hardware and an Internet connection. Many large corporations (I.e. IBM, AOL-Time Warner and HP/Compaq) are supporting the open source community leading to continued efforts and growth within this field. Together with the powerful tools and databases available over the Internet, biological computing has left the closed and limited community of well-funded organizations and is now widely available to the general public. Therefore, computational biology has been made highly accessible even for organizations with limited budgets.

However, bioinformatics research is still limited by the high cost of generating primary data in the laboratory, through conventional molecular biology methods and in particular through high throughput analyses, such as DNA microarrays, genomics and proteomics methods. Yet, this could lead to high specialization and efforts in poorly funded locations, such as third world countries, directed at problems specific to these locales, which in turn could lead to the development of highly skilled bioinformaticians that would be available for outsourced bioinformatics projects similar to what is currently occurring in the software industry.

References

[1] Somogyi R, Greller LD. (2001) The dynamics of molecular networks: applications to therapeutic discovery. *Drug Discov Today*, **6**, 1267–77.

[2] Ideker T, Galitski T, Hood L. (2001) A new approach to decoding life: systems biology. *Annu Rev Genomics Hum Genet*, **2:343-72.**, 343–72.

[3] Edwards JS, Ibarra RU, Palsson BO. (2001) In silico predictions of Escherichia coli metabolic capabilities are consistent with experimental data. *Nat Biotechnol*, **19**, 125–30.

[4] Galperin MY. (2004) The Molecular Biology Database Collection: 2004 update. *Nucleic Acids Res*, **32 Database issue:D3-22.**, D3–22.

[5] Matthiessen MW. (2003) BioWareDB: the biomedical software and database search engine. *Bioinformatics*, **19**, 2319–20.

[6] Stein LD. (2003) Integrating biological databases. *Nat Rev Genet*, **4**, 337–45.

[7] Dowell RD, Jokerst RM, Day A et al. (2001) The distributed annotation system. *BMC Bioinformatics*, **2**, 7.

[8] Wilkinson MD, Links M. (2002) BioMOBY: an open source biological web services proposal. *Brief Bioinform*, **3**, 331–41.

[9] Harris MA, Clark J, Ireland A et al. (2004) The Gene Ontology (GO) database and informatics resource. *Nucleic Acids Res*, **32 Database issue:D258-61.**, D258–D261.

[10] Spellman PT, Miller M, Stewart J et al. (2002) Design and implementation of microarray gene expression markup language (MAGE-ML). *Genome Biol*, **3**, RESEARCH0046.

[11] Smith RF, Wiese BA, Wojzynski MK et al. (1996) BCM Search Launcher– an integrated interface to molecular biology data base search and analysis services available on the World Wide Web. *Genome Res*, **6**, 454–62.

[12] Basu MK. (2001) SeWeR: a customizable and integrated dynamic HTML interface to bioinformatics services. *Bioinformatics*, **17**, 577–8.

[13] Subramaniam S. (1998) The Biology Workbench–a seamless database and analysis environment for the biologist. *Proteins*, **32**, 1–2.

[14] Berman HM, Westbrook J, Feng Z et al. (2000) The Protein Data Bank. *Nucleic Acids Res*, **28**, 235–42.

[15] Guex N, Peitsch MC. (1997) SWISS-MODEL and the Swiss-PdbViewer: an environment for comparative protein modeling. *Electrophoresis*, **18**, 2714–23.

[16] Bates PA, Kelley LA, MacCallum RM et al. (2001) Enhancement of protein modeling by human intervention in applying the automatic programs 3D-JIGSAW and 3D-PSSM. *Proteins*, **45 Suppl 5:39-46.**, 39–46.

[17] Mathews DH, Sabina J, Zuker M et al. (1999) Expanded sequence dependence of thermodynamic parameters improves prediction of RNA secondary structure. *J Mol Biol*, **288**, 911–40.

[18] Jr. SantaLucia J. (1998) A unified view of polymer, dumbbell, and oligonucleotide DNA nearest-neighbor thermodynamics. *Proc Natl Acad Sci U S A*, **95**, 1460–5.

[19] Breton V, Medina R, Montagnat J. (2003) DataGrid, prototype of a biomedical grid. *Methods Inf Med*, **42**, 143–7.

Index

A

adolescence, 115
amino acids, vii, ix, 1, 3, 6, 16, 20, 25, 29, 31, 39, 45, 61, 63, 64, 77, 88, 106, 107, 110, 136
antibody (Ab), 121
anticancer drug, 109
apoptosis, 12
arginine, 106

B

bacteria, 38, 88, 106, 107, 108, 117
bacterial, 51, 71, 106, 116
binding, 2, 5, 12, 13, 14, 19, 20, 22, 25, 26, 30, 37, 38, 39, 40, 51, 52, 55, 63, 64, 73, 74, 83, 84, 86, 93, 103, 111
biosynthesis, 56, 71, 93, 106, 107, 113
browser, 46, 47, 85, 136
browsing, 122, 135

C

calcium, 5, 14, 16, 20, 25, 105, 111
carbohydrate, 86
central nervous system (CNS), 104, 105
chemotaxis, 44, 52
chloroplast, 109, 115, 116, 117
chromosome, 88, 107, 109, 112
cloning, 68

cluster of differentiation (CD), 31, 137, 139
clustering, ix, 25, 60, 73, 93, 135, 137, 139
codon, 106
complementary DNA (cDNA), 92
computation, 30
connectivity, 112
cytochrome, 9, 15, 16, 19

D

data mining, 122
data structure, 122
dendritic cell (DC), 31, 33, 55, 91
differentiation, 3, 105
disease, 68, 69, 118
distributed computing, 139
DNA, ix, 2, 12, 19, 22, 25, 30, 38, 51, 52, 55, 80, 89, 100, 101, 105, 107, 109, 115, 116, 118, 119, 121, 122, 123, 126, 132, 135, 136, 140, 141
domain, viii, 12, 26, 34, 36, 37, 38, 45, 46, 48, 49, 51, 52, 53, 55, 56, 60, 61, 63, 65, 66, 68, 69, 70, 71, 72, 73, 74, 75, 76, 77, 79, 83, 84, 85, 86, 87, 91, 93, 111
drug design, 2

E

electrophoresis, 121
embryophyte, 96, 101
endocrine, 104

endogenous, 115
enzymatic activity, 63
enzymes, 2, 5, 12, 15, 19, 24, 30, 35, 38, 39,
　　45, 46, 54, 56, 57, 68, 83, 86, 107, 114, 135
eukaryote, 107, 113
eukaryotic cell, 109
evolution, 51, 72, 93, 95, 100, 103, 104, 105,
　　108, 110, 111, 112, 113, 114, 115, 116,
　　117, 118, 122
expressed sequence tag (EST), 105
extracellular, 111

F

factor i, 15, 21, 22, 60
false negative, 63
false positive, 12, 14, 17, 19, 21, 22, 24, 25,
　　30, 40, 63, 65, 101, 107
fatty acid, 19, 26
feedback, 74, 93
feedback inhibition, 74, 93
fermentation, 108
fungal, 108
fungus, 109

G

gene, 2, 24, 35, 38, 43, 45, 46, 49, 56, 57, 85,
　　90, 93, 95, 96, 98, 99, 100, 101, 102, 103,
　　104, 105, 106, 107, 108, 109, 110, 111,
　　112, 113, 114, 115, 116, 117, 118, 121,
　　123, 136, 141
gene expression, 141
gene transfer, 100, 102, 107, 109, 113, 114,
　　115, 116, 117, 118
genetic marker, 30
genome, vii, viii, ix, 3, 33, 34, 35, 43, 45, 48,
　　49, 56, 57, 60, 71, 72, 75, 87, 89, 91, 92,
　　94, 95, 96, 97, 100, 101, 102, 103, 105,
　　106, 107, 109, 111, 112, 113, 114, 115,
　　117, 118, 119, 121, 123, 136
genotype, 30
glatiramer acetate (GA), 31, 117, 118
glucose, 76, 108
glycoprotein, 104

growth factors, 37, 38, 55

H

heme, 12, 19
heterocyst, 52
heterotrophic, 107
histidine, 51, 52
HIV-1, 13
hormones, 104, 108
human immunodeficiency virus (HIV), 13
hypothesis, 103, 115, 116

I

immune system, 104
immunity, 103, 104
immunoglobulin (Ig), 103
inflammatory disease, 121
innate immunity, 104
insulin, 37, 55, 83, 84
intercellular, 103, 109
interfaces, 19, 24, 30, 46, 122, 123, 127
Internet, 119, 120, 132, 135, 136, 137, 138,
　　139, 140
intravenous (IV), vii, viii, 63, 95
intron, 108, 113, 135
invertebrate, 103
ion channels, 14, 19, 30
iron, 41
isolation, viii, 60

L

lactate dehydrogenase, 15
leptin, 111, 113, 114, 115
linkage, 101
lipid, 19

M

major histocompatibility complex (MHC), 12,
　　13
mammal, 96
mammalian brain, 105

mammals, 97, 104
matrix, 57, 64, 110
messenger RNA (mRNA), 112, 122
metabolism, 52, 112, 117, 121
mitochondria, 108, 109, 113
modelling, 64, 70
modules, 51, 86
molecule, vii, 1, 18, 20
mRNA, 112
mutations, 20, 66, 99, 107, 114, 122
myoglobin, 11, 14, 15, 16, 19

N

nematodes, 106
nervous system, 103, 104
network, viii, 33, 36, 43, 72, 73, 112, 113,
    117, 118, 120, 121, 135, 136, 139, 140
neurotransmitter, 105
nicotine, 105
nodes, 72, 85, 101
nuclear receptors, 104
nucleic acid, 80
nucleotide, 80, 110, 117, 122
nucleus, 95, 109, 115, 116, 117

O

obesity, 111, 114
olfactory, 104, 114
operating system, 120, 121, 132, 137
operon, 48, 49, 56
organelles, 109, 116
organism, 2, 45, 88, 99, 100, 102, 112
oxygen, 107

P

parasite, 114
parvalbumin, 4, 5, 8, 11, 15, 16, 17, 18, 19,
    20, 21, 26, 28, 30
pathogenesis, 60
peptidase, 93
performance, 66
phenotype, 30

phenylalanine, 74, 93
phosphates, 26
phosphorylation, 5
placenta, 111
plants, 38, 105, 106, 108, 109, 112, 113, 115,
    118
plasmid, 108
plastid, 109
polymerase, 100
polymerase chain reaction (PCR), 121, 135,
    136
polymorphisms, 122
polypeptide, 5
potassium, 93
primate, 111, 116
probability, 60, 61, 62
proliferation, ix
protease, 111
protein family, viii, 34, 44, 46, 54, 56, 60, 61,
    63, 77, 84, 86, 87, 92
protein synthesis, 7
proteomics, ix, 89, 123

Q

queuing systems, 82

R

receptors, 67, 68, 83, 84, 104, 110, 111, 114,
    115, 117, 118
recombination, 100
regulators, 48, 49, 51, 52, 53
retrieval, iv, 73, 75
retrovirus, 115
ribosome, 29
RNA, vii, 1, 2, 31, 51, 80, 99, 121, 122, 135,
    136, 141
rodents, 104

S

seed, 45, 46, 47, 66, 69, 70, 73, 76
self-organizing, ix
sensitivity, 57, 63, 64, 65

security, 124
server, 80, 81, 82, 123, 135, 136, 139
software, ix, 5, 62, 77, 81, 82, 88, 119, 120, 121, 123, 124, 125, 126, 127, 129, 132, 133, 135, 137, 139, 140
solution, 60, 123
species, 38, 68, 71, 85, 96, 98, 100, 101, 102, 105, 107, 108, 109, 110, 111, 112
specificity, 63, 65, 66
sperm, 116
steroid, 104
stimulus, 51
survival, x, 99, 102, 120

T

taxonomy, 43, 45, 46, 47, 85
telomere, 71
thesaurus, 126
thiamin, 56
threshold, 63, 65, 75, 101
thyroglobulin, 38
thyroid, 104
tissues, 99, 108
topology, 103
tracking, 138
transcription, 52, 102, 107, 112
transduction, 49, 51, 52, 53, 56, 57
transfer, 95, 107, 108, 109, 113, 114, 115, 116, 117, 135
translation, 102, 135
treatment, 111

trees, 75, 101, 109, 110
tryptophan, 74
tyrosine, 74

V

variance, 110
vascular, 108
vertebrates, 38, 96, 103, 104, 108, 114, 115, 117
viruses, 88

W

web, 70, 71, 80, 123, 135, 138, 139, 141
web pages, 70, 71
web service, 123, 141
websites, 86
workflow, 132, 133
workstations, 120

X

XML, x, 82, 119, 124

Y

yeast, 106, 110, 112, 117, 118

Z

zinc, 103